Greetings!

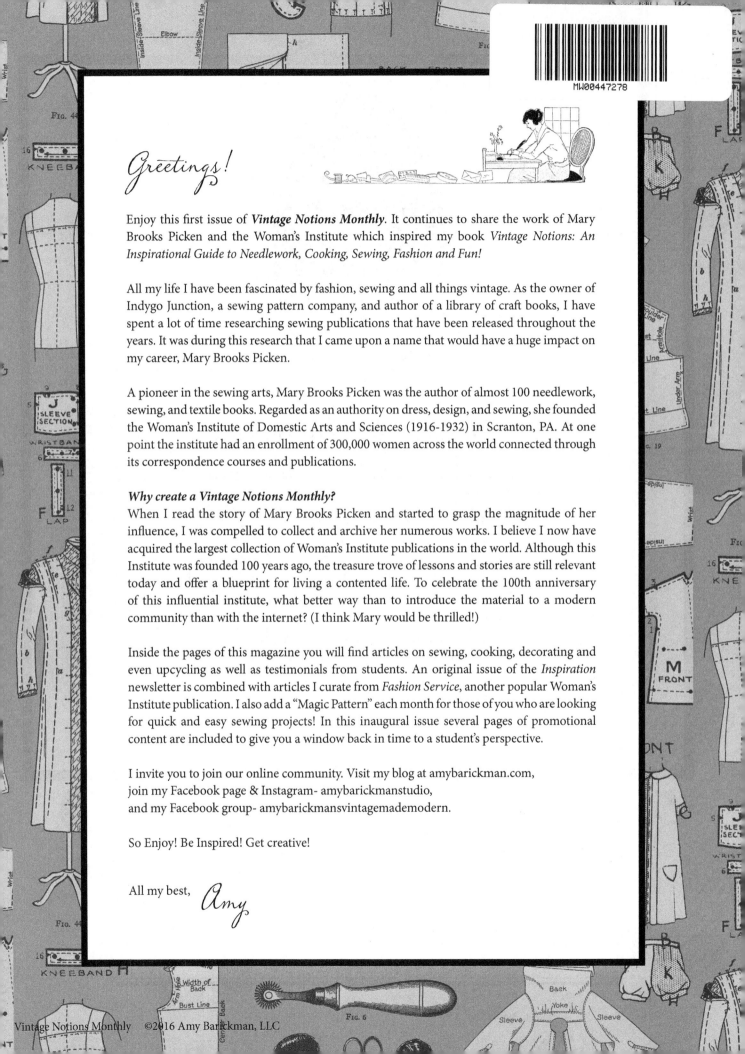

Enjoy this first issue of *Vintage Notions Monthly*. It continues to share the work of Mary Brooks Picken and the Woman's Institute which inspired my book *Vintage Notions: An Inspirational Guide to Needlework, Cooking, Sewing, Fashion and Fun!*

All my life I have been fascinated by fashion, sewing and all things vintage. As the owner of Indygo Junction, a sewing pattern company, and author of a library of craft books, I have spent a lot of time researching sewing publications that have been released throughout the years. It was during this research that I came upon a name that would have a huge impact on my career, Mary Brooks Picken.

A pioneer in the sewing arts, Mary Brooks Picken was the author of almost 100 needlework, sewing, and textile books. Regarded as an authority on dress, design, and sewing, she founded the Woman's Institute of Domestic Arts and Sciences (1916-1932) in Scranton, PA. At one point the institute had an enrollment of 300,000 women across the world connected through its correspondence courses and publications.

Why create a Vintage Notions Monthly?

When I read the story of Mary Brooks Picken and started to grasp the magnitude of her influence, I was compelled to collect and archive her numerous works. I believe I now have acquired the largest collection of Woman's Institute publications in the world. Although this Institute was founded 100 years ago, the treasure trove of lessons and stories are still relevant today and offer a blueprint for living a contented life. To celebrate the 100th anniversary of this influential institute, what better way than to introduce the material to a modern community than with the internet? (I think Mary would be thrilled!)

Inside the pages of this magazine you will find articles on sewing, cooking, decorating and even upcycling as well as testimonials from students. An original issue of the *Inspiration* newsletter is combined with articles I curate from *Fashion Service*, another popular Woman's Institute publication. I also add a "Magic Pattern" each month for those of you who are looking for quick and easy sewing projects! In this inaugural issue several pages of promotional content are included to give you a window back in time to a student's perspective.

I invite you to join our online community. Visit my blog at amybarickman.com, join my Facebook page & Instagram- amybarickmanstudio, and my Facebook group- amybarickmansvintagemademodern.

So Enjoy! Be Inspired! Get creative!

All my best, *Amy*

Our Fourth Anniversary

RESPLENDENT with the good it is disseminating to womankind, the Woman's Institute enters into its fifth year of usefulness. From one student, on February 29, 1916, it has grown steadily until today its students number fifty thousand. With the doctrine of "helping women to help themselves" as its guiding force, the Institute hopes to expand and grow and ever be an influence for good in the lives of all women — a medium through which every woman, no matter where she may live, may acquire that knowledge which will serve her well in every way.

—*Mary Brooks Picken*

The image you see above was the original cover for this issue of Inspiration from February 1920, celebrating it's fourth anniversary. I chose to update the cover for a more modern look using a cover from the Winter 1925-26 issue of Fashion Service.

A *Letter* From Mrs. Picken

MY DEAR AUNT:

Your letter—what joy it gave me! Just to know that you are interested in me and in my work is itself an inspiration. And, do you know, sometimes I feel that your heart and spirit are in the work along with mine, for, after all, you and grand-mother were my first teachers.

When you taught me the meaning of warp and woof and how to know the dif-ference between linen and cotton and how to tie a tailor's knot—and the many hun-dred facts about domestic arts—I am sure neither of you realized how very far that instruction would carry.

YOU say, "I hear so much about the Institute—tell me exactly what it is, and please be specific because I want to know the whole story." I shall try to tell you all, but I would much rather have you come and see for yourself, because in correspon-dence instruction there is so much that is fine that one cannot exactly express.

Goethe says: "A book allowed me to pause at a passage, and even to look back, which is impossible with oral delivery or a teacher." And so it is with correspondence instruction. One can pause, digest at will, and apply at pleasure, and in this way actually make the knowledge a part of one-self. Although you did not realize it, you were a correspondence teacher, for I have many of your precious letters, each giving me information that you thought I espe-cially required. Your love made it possible for you to write those letters, but only a few of us were fortunate enough to benefit by your store of knowledge.

OFTEN in my work here, I receive letters from girls and women asking me whether I believe they can learn to make their own clothes or to sew professionally. I repeat to them what you have so often told me: "It depends on you and your own mental and physical attitude toward the task. Aimless performance never brought success to any one, but a definite ideal and a sincere purpose will always bring a true realization of the goal."

And in thinking about this advice of yours, which I have remembered this long time, it often, almost unconsciously, brings to mind the old hymn:

Prayer is the heart's sincere desire,
Uttered or unexpressed—
The motion of a hidden fire
That trembles in each breast.

In my work with students, I realize more definitely the necessity of their kindling a fire of desire and of having it blaze forth into a sincere effort for accomplishment.

YOU will recall that when I began to teach sewing in the classroom I resented the limitations of that plan of teaching. We could help splendidly those who came to us, but the tragedy of it was we were

For this anniversary issue of INSPIRATION, we asked Mrs. Picken to write an article that would set forth the ideals and objects of the Institute from her point of view. This she has done so well in a letter to one of her aunts that we are repro-ducing it just as she has written it.—EDITOR.

not reaching those who most needed the help. We find that hundreds of women do not appreciate how much they need to learn to sew until the trousseau is to be made, or the baby's layette, and when these personal problems do come it is too late to get the training for the task.

It is these very women that the Institute serves. Just now it is our joy and privi-lege to be helping more than 50,000 women in just this way, and upwards of two hundred new ones start with us every day, so you see our family is really growing very fast.

The average age of our students is 26 years. Out of every hundred, 58 are home women, 20 professional dressmakers, 15 teachers, and the remaining 7 represent every manner of occupation. But the age will tell you the story. Our work is chiefly for those who no longer have school privi-leges and who need to learn to do their individual tasks in order to make life sweeter and bigger and finer for the loved ones whose very fate they hold.

AND there you have the secret of our suc-cess. The Institute has grown far beyond our happiest dreams. It is heralded every-where for the good it is accomplishing, and the reason is that those who enroll for our studies are serious-minded women, eager for self-advancement, patient, persistent, and with a sense for responsibilities that makes it possible for our instruction to go deep and do its greatest work. And the sincerity of our students is our instructors' greatest inspiration. The fine, splendid type of women we serve makes cooperation entirely practical and keenly desired.

The Woman's Institute is almost four years old, but it seems the idea of it must have been always, for through its channels women are brought close together, "the right kind of vanity is cultivated," and their hands, heart, and brain are taught to work in unison.

I HAVE often wished that you could en-roll for our studies just to see how our work is taken care of, for you of all women would appreciate and understand it.

I should like to take you through our many departments, that you might see from the very beginning how a woman becomes interested, a student, an enthusiastic worker, and, finally, a graduate. She first becomes interested in our service through our magazine announcements or acquaint-ance with an Institute student. She writes for information about a particular Course. Upon receiving it, she decides to become a student and sends us her application for membership. We send her a letter and her

first lessons. She studies and sends us written answers to questions asked and sampler stitches and seams showing what she is able to accomplish and then, on and on, each lesson representing steps of progress that make for perfection.

YOU would admire the type of young women who take care of Institute les-sons and letters. They are all so wholly fine—they must have a domestic instinct, they must be sympathetic, they must be tolerant, and they must have sufficient edu-cation to use good judgment. We have a technical requirement of at least a high-school training, while more than 40 per cent. of our staff of over 400 have a college or a normal-school education or its equiv-alent. The majority can cook well and many of them can sew with skill and can create really beautiful things. So, you see, they are a band of well-trained helpers, and it is a joy to work with them because of their acute appreciation of the service the Institute continually strives to render.

AND with them one feels safe, because when a student comes to us with her work—in many cases she has never sewed before, and perhaps her first work is very crude—her stitches and seams are care-fully examined and if need be sampler stitches and seams of our own making are sent to her so that we may be assured that she has a correct understanding.

If the student evidences sewing knowl-edge at the very outset, we help her to get a broader, bigger grasp and speed her on to the advanced work where every problem will be one of pertinent benefit.

SO, YOU see, the Institute provides much for every woman, and the knowledge is so imme-diately applicable that the study is not tedious.

I almost jumped when I wrote that word *tedious*, for I fear any one else reading this letter would think it a bit so; but you, dear aunt, have always lis-tened so patiently to my joys and sorrows, and I'm sure you will under-stand my great enthu-siasm. For years I have been hoping and planning for our Institute stu-dents, and as I see my dreams being realized it makes me very happy. I'm glad you asked for this let-ter, because I feel that you, like the folks at home, should know all about that which means so much to me.

Affectionately your

MARY

Keeping Pace With the *Growing Girl*

By ALWILDA FELLOWS
Department of Dressmaking

ISN'T it a real problem to keep on hand an ample supply of frocks to meet the every-day, as well as the occasional, needs of the growing girl? Truly, her requirements are quite exacting, in most instances above the level of her mother's and surely not so far below the level of her grown-up sister's, on whom, according to the very youthful and consequently disregarded opinion, the attention of the family seems to be focused.

Such an opinion, formed as it is through observation, is generally justified. Doesn't mother spend every possible minute, sometimes extending these minutes well along into the night, in an effort to keep Miss 16-to-20's clothes up to date as to style and the occasions for which they are needed? Doesn't father frequently fret about the extravagant and pleasure-bent tendencies of the new generation? And doesn't big brother, who recently returned to civil life, although the most wonderful hero in the world, have a most exasperating manner of entirely overlooking the very occasional instances when his younger sister wears an exceptionally pretty new hat or frock, and, on the other hand, fairly swell up with pride each time older sister appears in a new outfit—occasions that are by no means rare?

BUT here I am commenting on the very subject from which I should try to draw attention. I'm agreeing with the small girl just at present, and I certainly would like to plan for her some little frocks that would compare most favorably with those in her older sister's wardrobe. If, in this planning, I embody practical details that will not only make her mother's work on the garments a real pleasure, but also insure lasting satisfaction, my object will be fully accomplished.

Just at the present time, styles for women are not settled, and because of this very fact, now is an excellent time to work on children's garments, anticipate all their spring and early summer needs, and thus, later on, have sufficient time to make satisfactorily the apparel required for the older members of the family.

FOR several seasons past, simplicity has been the keynote in children's styles. Little dresses have been built on practically straight lines and have depended almost entirely on unusual features in their cut for distinctiveness and style effect. Spring styles emphasize these very points perhaps more strongly than ever. But for novelty, there are many unusual designing features noted and hand embroidery is employed in such attractive, even though

simple, ways that the little garments are far from ordinary.

Take, for example, the tiny frock shown at the upper left, which is a *Fashion Review* style. It is distinctive in every sense of the word, and yet its development is very simple. As illustrated, it is made of two colors of linen, one a pretty, soft shade of yellow and the other hyacinth, a new combination that is particularly effective. The embroidery on both the yellow and the lavender is in self-color. The design is a conventional rose developed in the outlining-stitch, wool floss being used for this purpose.

Two harmonizing shades of chambray or cotton poplin, such as tan with green or white with pink, blue, green, or lavender, might be combined very effectively in a similar design, provided the conventional embroidery design were omitted and the battlement effect blanket-stitched in heavy mercerized floss of the same color as that used for the upper part of the dress, or the joining finished with machine hem-stitching. In this case, the sleeve, also, might be finished in battlement effect.

To form a pattern for this design, use a plain one-piece dress pattern that you have found satisfactory. Outline on this the battlement effect and the low, round-neck line with its slashed sides, and cut the pattern on the line marked for the battlement effect. In using these separate pattern sections, be sure to make allowance for seams beyond the cut edges.

The slashes at the neck line make unnecessary an opening at the center back. To finish these slashes, place a piece of material over each, stitch inside the slashed edges, and then turn the facing piece to the wrong side, trim away the surplus material, and secure the facing with tiny stitches.

GREEN-CHECKED gingham can make itself very useful for trimming, as is evidenced by the *Royal* design shown at the right in the center. This is applied in scallop effect to chambray of a matching shade of green. White piqué in a very fine quality might be used as a substitute for the checked trimming, provided the scallops were made of only one thickness of material and the edges picoted. Double scallops of white organdie suggest still another possibility in trimming.

A plain-kimono dress pattern may form the foundation for this style. Outline on it the short-waist effect and the extensions from this waist at the side front. Use only the waist and side extension pattern in cutting the material. For the skirt, cut straight widths. Do not trim away the material underneath the extended portions of the waist; rather, permit these extensions to fall free and face them with lawn or self-material.

ANTICIPATION of warm spring days and the many occasions incident to their arrival that will require just the nicest kind of dress, brings to mind that much-favored fabric, organdie. Is there anything more appropriate as an expression of youth than an organdie frock ruffled in the daintiest imaginable fashion?

If made of white organdie, the *Royal* party frock shown at the left in the central illustration might have ruffles of the same material in a pastel shade, such as pink, blue, green, lavender, or yellow, and a matching color of ribbon for a sash. Colored organdie used for the body of the dress would require ruffles in the same color. The contrast in color may, in this instance, be afforded merely by a sash of novelty or picoted ribbon.

THE best means of disproving the theory concerning the "awkward age" is to provide for the girl who will soon enter her teens garments that are so quietly attractive and individually becoming that she is bound to feel and act quite at ease when wearing them. Needless to say, simplicity should dominate in such styles, a typical example of which is shown by the *Royal* design at the lower right. This frock would be attractive if developed in chambray, imitation linen, linen, crêpe de Chine, taffeta, or a soft woolen material, the fabric being regulated by the

purpose for which the dress is intended. The smocking, as well as the blanket-stitching used to accentuate the panel effect, may be done in mercerized, silk, or wool floss, according to the material used.

A WORD in regard to coats for children. For the most part they are replicas of styles for grown-ups. If any difference is noted, it is generally a more marked simplicity in the styles for children. This is typical of even the designs for very young children. The dressier model of silk that was trimmed in some elaborate fashion has been supplanted by sports styles.

Polo cloth is a fabric that is being featured for children as well as for misses and women. Coats of this type are generally made in three-quarter length.

Checked velour, principally in black and white, is shown to a very great extent. New York shops offer this particular material in a variety of ways. One very unusual model has brown leather collar, cuffs, and pocket flaps. Another has a vest and collar of red broadcloth. But, regardless of the effectiveness of these models, velours in plain colors are reported to find more ready sale. Other popular fabrics are soft weaves of the velour type, wool jersey, and tricotine, which is particularly good in capes.

These various materials depend to a great extent on their cut to express their individuality. Box plaits arranged in various ways detract in a very pleasing manner from the severe simplicity of the backs of some models, while fancy pockets accomplish this same purpose in the front.

YOU may be interested to know that the vogue of capes for children is by no means a past number. Last year the becomingness and the desirability of cape styles for the juvenile were quite forcibly impressed, with the result that a greater variety of styles are offered this year. However, capes are not exactly practical for very cold weather unless a coat or sweater is worn underneath, and, for this reason, the season for capes is not here.

Interesting Millinery Items

By MARY MAHON
Department of Millinery

UNLESS it is the chirping of the first robin, no other sign of spring causes so much delight as the first glimpse of spring millinery in the shop windows. Who has not experienced pleasant little thrills upon seeing the new and pretty hats that are put on display in the early spring and that possess all possible loveliness and attractiveness? While the winter chill is still in the air, milady, although wrapped in furs, is often enticed by the showing of pretty hats, and every clever planner gets from window displays valuable hints of approaching styles and suggestions that will help her to decide on her spring attire and in many cases enable her, by a little fixing, to bring her last year's hat up to date.

THE predominating feature for the coming season is the hand-made hat, and of course this means that fabrics of all kinds will be used. There are so many beautiful fabrics to be had these days that it is difficult to know just where to begin to describe them. Highly lacquered and brilliant materials are very evident in the new showings. For instance, there is satin and moiré cire, which means waxed and which spells the dominant note in spring millinery, for everything—straws, wings, flowers, and ribbons—is waxed. Foremost in favor in the luster-bright millinery ideas is celaphone. This material comes in long strips that resemble gelatine sheets, and it can be used in various ways, such as in the making of solid hats, for trimming hats, and in preparing any number of attractive forms of fringes, bands, strands, and even pretty flowers. It seems certain that celaphone and its kindred gelatinous effects will continue in favor throughout the season.

A MATERIAL that was used extensively last season and is now coming in for a great share of favor is leather in the form of kid, suède, and "toile cire," which is really a light-weight oilcloth that resembles patent leather very closely. Brocaded Batavia is another attractive novelty cloth that promises to be very popular, as it is a very desirable material for draping turbans and for fitting broad-brimmed hats. The colorful embroidery designs are done in raffia and are made so solid that they reveal very little of the foundation material.

A very new effect is produced in the trimming of these fabric hats by means of tortoise shell and isinglass novelties in beads, fringes, and ornaments. In some cases, the ornaments are used on the under brim of a small drooping hat, giving a decided Egyptian effect. Such a hat is worn very low over the ears and eyes, showing very little, if any, hair.

THE staple colors this season are brown, black, and navy, but there are many new tones that are positively adorable. One shade that seems to be irresistible and to take entire possession of one is jade. Then, too, the rainbow in iridescent effect is a decidedly new achievement in millinery, many beautiful effects being produced through the clever ingenuity of the milliner by simply placing one shade of maline over a fabric of another shade. One particularly good result is obtained by using navy-blue maline over gold taffeta.

Another interesting color is Kelly green. We are just beginning to appreciate what an exquisite color this is, especially when it is brought out in this season's materials or combined with patent leather.

ONE of the best models for the coming season is a sailor having a brim 2 inches wide and a crown 4½ or 5 inches high and fitted plain with patent leather or black oilcloth. The edge of the brim is bound in Kelly green, No. 2 faille silk ribbon stitched with raffia being used. The side crown is embroidered elaborately in cire raffia of many vivid colors beautifully blended. The only trimming is a band of the No. 2 ribbon drawn around the crown and finished with a bow at the front. This particular hat is especially good because it can be worn by so many different types.

ANOTHER item in millinery that deserves considerable thought is the veil, which, although formerly considered a separate article to be worn only on occasions, has been discovered by art to be the accessory that completes the attire of the well-dressed woman. The veils for this season are of all kinds and hues, from the fine-mesh, closely tucked-in veil to the gorgeous flowing one that falls over the shoulders to the waist line. The Chantilly lace veil is greatly in evidence, as are also many ornate nets, which produce decidedly pretty effects, especially when used over a fascinating hat made entirely of flowers. When used with such a hat, the veil will greatly enhance the color scheme if it is of a different hue from the colors in the flowers.

In addition to putting the finishing touch to milady's toilet or producing a certain effect in colors, a veil brings much comfort to the wearer by keeping her troublesome stray locks in their proper place.

Edited by GUSTAVE L. WEINSS

The Spirit of *Greatness*

BY THE EDITOR

FEBRUARY is the month when the Institute celebrates the anniversary of its origin. This year, on our fourth birthday, we have much over which to rejoice, for have not our students grown in numbers to 50,000? And do we not realize that our usefulness as an institution is recognized and appreciated by ever-increasing numbers of earnest, wide-awake women—women who understand the problems that confront them and are big enough to let us help them solve these problems?

IF YOU were to ask me, "To what do you attribute the wonderful growth of the Institute?" I should reply, "To the spirit of greatness that underlies its very existence, to that real desire to serve which permeates the very atmosphere of the Institute."

Now by greatness I do not mean the self-aggrandizement—the puffed-up feeling—that may come as a result of having performed some laudable act or deed, but that greatness which Emerson meant when he said, " 'Tis the spirit of greatness which builds intitutions that deal with humanities," that indescribable something which seems to govern the acts of those who wish to serve their fellow beings. "Count that person great," says the philosopher, "who aspires not to glory, but to service. True greatness comes not from without, but from within."

SO, IN this birthday talk about the Institute, I should be negligent indeed if I did not express appreciation of our Vice-President and Director of Instruction—Mary Brooks Picken.

Our thousands of students know her through their lessons and their correspondence with her, but here at the Institute we know her by personal contact and in this way understand that to her is due the spirit that dominates the Institute. Indeed, just as you as students know that she believes color, line, and fabric to be the real essentials of dress, so do we know that she believes courtesy, fair dealing, and service to be the keynote of her relationship to her students. So, you see, you have, as the dominating spirit of the Institute, a champion of your rights.

IT SEEMS like only a few short months instead of years that Mrs. Picken came to Scranton from her native state—Kansas. There, nurtured among people who have a reputation for doing things not for themselves alone but for the good of all, she saw the need of educating women to be industrious and independent, she recognized the importance of teaching women in and out of the home the domestic arts and sciences, and, greater yet, she had a vision of the way in which these things could be made to come to pass and thus benefit all women wherever they may chance to dwell. O, yes; the Woman's Institute is older in thought than in reality.

IT WOULD be too long a story to tell of how Mrs. Picken set about to prepare herself for the life task she chose for herself, or to enter into the details of how she brought into existence the Institute, which has proved, is proving, and will continue to prove a blessing to every woman and girl who will profit by its courses of study. Suffice it to say that through her earnest effort and initiative, her tireless energy and practical knowledge, her sympathetic understanding of the needs of women, she made a way, and today—well, notwithstanding the fact that she has been directly instrumental in brightening the lives of so many, many women, she is still planning and preparing to expand the Institute and make it a greater power for good.

OFTEN, when I have heard of the success of persons who have had visions of great things, I have wondered how it must feel to have won. But my almost daily association with Mrs. Picken has taught me how I should behave. I should try to cultivate the modesty she possesses and to become saturated with the spirit of service for my fellow beings which she constantly displays by word and deed, for I know that genuine greatness consists in modesty and service. Then, as she does, I should try to instil these same qualities into my associates, for I now know that " 'Tis the spirit of greatness which builds institutions that deal with humanities."

The *Extra Day* of 1920

By LAURA MacFARLANE
Editorial Department

WHEN Leap Year comes along with its extra day in February and the first of March "leaps over" one day additional, we get the idea that something unusual is going to happen and we become filled with a feeling of expectancy. Usually, however, this year means nothing more to the average individual than the surrendering, on the part of the male sex, of their right to make all advances and the transferring of this privilege to the members of the fair sex. When Cupid's arrows go whizzing by, we like to fancy that their destination is reversed and, instead of arousing the affections of the girl we have noticed so often in the company of a certain young man, they are directed by her and are intended to make a mortal stab in his quick-throbbing heart.

BUT be such fancies as they may, the extra day that the calendar makers provided to come once in every four years sometimes has a deeper significance, and such we find is the case with the Woman's Institute. Just four years ago the 29th of this month, as practically all of you know, we came into being by enrolling our first student, and from that day on we have had such a phenomenal growth that it has been a hard matter for us to restrain ourselves until our first birthday arrived so that we could show our appreciation in some fitting manner. And now, after waiting and planning

and rejoicing, we come to our natal day only to find that it falls on Sunday, and in respect for the day we shall have to defer our real birthday festivities until some later time.

Leap-Year Day Dinner

Chicken Broth

Salted Wafers   Celery   Pickles

Roast Lamb

Mint Jelly   Gravy

Mashed Potatoes   Scalloped Brussels Sprouts

Pineapple and Banana Salad   Cheese Wafers

French Vanilla Ice Cream   White Cake

Coffee   Bonbons   Salted Nuts

HOWEVER, we need not let the day pass without marking it in some way. Sunday being the one day of the week when the home circle is usually completed, what would be more fitting than to take greater pains than usual with the Sunday dinner and provide a repast that will be at once dainty and appetizing? This will probably be the order of the day all over the land, but in the families of Institute members, this especially planned Sunday dinner will have a double significance.

WITH this thought in mind, I have prepared a menu that I am sure will prove a most delectable one if care is used in its preparation. If it is not possible to procure the food called for in some of the dishes, others may, of course, be substituted, provided attention is given to the proper balancing of the meal. For instance, if Brussels sprouts should not be obtainable, carrots and peas or cauliflower would make a very good substitute.

For the salad suggested, a sweet dressing in which pineapple juice forms the foundation and whipped cream is added for delicacy, will be found delicious. Large white cherries may be substituted for the slices of banana if they should be preferred.

In this day of high prices, it may seem an extravagance to have French vanilla ice cream because of the number of eggs required in its preparation, and yet when you consider that only the yolks go into the ice cream and the whites may be used for your cake, which may be angel food or merely a white butter cake that the family like, the dessert selected is not an extravagance after all. And is not this meal to be served on the odd day of the year, when, if ever, we might feel free to allow ourselves a little license in the way of our food so long as we still keep within the bounds of our resources?

After the *Day's Work*

By MAX EHRMANN

AFTER the day's work, in the quiet night, sit care free, relaxed, and silent. With the silver threads of memory and the gold threads of hope weave a fabric of wholesome dreams. If you are old, perhaps you will tell yourself the story of by-gone happy times with friends—maybe with some one you loved. You may recall the nights with the big stars and the gold-burnished moon, and the wonder that it was to be young. With gentle hands, memory will soften the picture, and the delights of other years will live in you again.

IF YOU are young, you will paint a picture of the dream of hope. Hope is the helmsman of the phantom ship of life. It sings as the sirens sang. Hope is a whisper in a waking dream, a spirit hand that beckons, a voice that says, "Come." Like love, it is the sunlight of the soul, the rose of the springtime of the world within. Hope says to fancy, "Show me the heights that I shall climb; and light up, if but for a moment, the chambers of my future palace."

IF YOU are young, you will paint a picture of the dream of hope. And as you sit in the quiet night, you will be the thing you crave to be, sail the seas you yearn to sail, and know the love your heart would know.

And on the morrow, when you build in the world of contending men, you may make a thing that is real of the picture of your dream. Therefore, that you may rest and hear the luring whispers of hope, coming like distant music, in the quiet night sit care free, relaxed, and silent.

Let us hope that one day all mankind will be happy and wise; and, though this day never should dawn, to have hoped for it cannot be wrong. And, in any event, it is helpful to speak of happiness to those who are sad, that thus at least they may learn what it is that happiness means.—MAURICE MAETERLINCK.

Woman's Institute *Question-Box*

Taffeta in Favor

What kind of silk would you suggest for my Easter dress? I should like to obtain something that will give good service. M. J. K.

Just one glance at the personal information you sent to us after you enrolled, brought to my mind brown taffeta as the most suitable material for your new frock. I am suggesting brown, not merely because it is one of the most popular colors, especially in taffeta, but more particularly because I am sure it will prove very becoming to you. And, as for taffeta, well, this seems to be the thought uppermost in the minds of designers and consequently taffeta is used in dresses for women, misses, and children.

We have become a little dubious of taffeta, I realize, but at present this is made in very soft, excellent qualities, unweighted and unadulterated; therefore, if a good quality of this material is chosen it will surely prove serviceable.

A word in regard to brown—the mere mention of brown taffeta may bring to mind a very ordinary appearing dress. But this season's brown is far from lifeless. Instead, it is rich in tone, quite different from the somber brown taffeta of our grandmother's day.

Your age is another reason for my suggestion in regard to taffeta. This material is generally considered more "youthful" in appearance than satin and therefore more suitable for a young woman. If you select a style having a slightly bouffant effect in the skirt, a low-waisted, rather softly crushed bodice effect and short kimono sleeves, I am sure you will be delighted with the result.

Notes on Lesson Reports

I made a request for some samples of material on my last lesson report to you, and afterwards I wondered whether it wouldn't have been better to make such a request on a separate sheet of paper. Which way do you prefer? H. E. H.

A separate sheet of paper of course would have been better. Students should use their answer paper for answering their Examination Questions and their Information Blanks when asking for information about their lessons. If you send all your communications to us on paper separate from your answer sheets, you may be assured of the highest grade of service. By so doing your inquiries will be sent directly to the department that is best prepared to take care of them, and thus attention may be given to them at the same time your lesson reports are being taken care of in the Instruction Department.

Popularity of Satine

In many fashion notes I have read that satine will be a popular spring fabric. Is this material the same as that we have been using for lining, underskirts, etc.? If so, do you consider it suitable for children's clothes? E. S.

The satine that is now given prominence is nothing more than that once "lowly" fabric made in a particularly good quality. Several New York shops that maintain very excellent children's departments are featuring satine. The little dresses made of this material are many of them simple in line, dark in color, and appliquéd with quaint figures in contrasting colors. For instance, a black satine dress is appliquéd with designs in rose and worn with rose satine bloomers.

An especially popular model is in pink satine with bloomers of self-color or of black. Two styles of bloomers are shown, straight pantalettes and those shirred and trimmed with ruffles of lace. The latter type is very quaint in appearance, suggestive of styles worn many, many years ago.

Printed satine in pale colors, pink, blue, and lavender, is somewhat newer than the plain fabric. This, also, is developed in designs suggestive of olden times. Frills of batiste are used for the neck and sleeve trimmings of many of these models, and a band of this same material is sometimes introduced at the waist line.

Most of the satine dresses are really very pretty and to say the least chic, as well as serviceable.

Satine is also being used for misses and women's dresses and will, without doubt, become quite popular.

Want to Get Acquainted?

The following Institute students desire to become acquainted with other Institute students residing in their localities:

New Bedford, Massachusetts............M. E. C.
Boonville, New York.....................M. C.
Forth Worth, Texas.....................I. M. M.
Chicago Heights, Illinois................H. McC.
Marshfield, Wisconsin ....F. W.
Albany, New York.......................E. M. T.
Winchester, Virginia ....W. E. A.
Biddeford, or Saco, Maine..............M. J. P.
United States or Canada................R. O.
Atascadero, California ....L. A. M.
Uniontown, Pennsylvania ....A. L. S.
Braddock, Pennsylvania ....J. K.

I should like to correspond with some of the Institute students taking the Dressmaking Course, who are about my age, which is 19 years. J. G.

I should like to become acquainted with another student of about 15 years of age, who is taking the Complete Dressmaking Course. S. H.

I should like to become acquainted with a student residing in the Northwest section of Washington, District of Columbia, taking the Dressmaking Course. F. S.

I should like to hear from some of the girls, who are about 18 years of age, taking the Dressmaking Course. S. B.

I should like to correspond with any student taking Dressmaking and Tailoring. E. S.

I should like to get acquainted with some of the students taking the Dressmaking Course. R. K.

I should like to secure a place as helper to a dressmaker. M. S.

If other Woman's Institute students would like to get in touch with the inquiring students, we shall be glad to supply the names and addresses.

Suit Materials and Colors

What colors and materials are being used for spring suits? I should like to know, particularly, whether navy-blue serge is at all favored. I really prefer this to any other color and material for I find it so very satisfactory. E. V. F.

Blue serge is holding its own remarkably well. A great many of the newest spring models feature this material, as well as those other well-liked fabrics, tricotine and gabardine of fine weave. Tweeds are shown in a variety of colors, henna, gray, jade, and light sand predominating. Heather mixtures are quite new and already very popular—the brown and tan tones are especially good in this fabric. Soft woolen materials having a suggestion of a nap are used for rather dressy models. These are shown principally in bright blues, spring grays, and tans of various shades.

Suits for sports wear are in many instances of bright color; new shades, such as an odd red, green in water shades, hyacinth, and bright, unusual blues, are noted.

Samplers Sent for Reference

We appreciate the response to our recent appeal for the return of samplers, and we take this opportunity to thank those who returned the samplers they had. There are, however, many more to be returned. As there is urgent need of these samplers, we are making another appeal to students who have finished with the samplers sent to them by the Institute. Won't you kindly return them, so that they may go to the aid of other students?

Chocolate-Coated Raisins

I noticed in December INSPIRATION a discussion on how to coat candies with chocolate. Are chocolate-coated raisins prepared in the same way? I am very fond of these and should appreciate a recipe for them. E. B.

The method used to coat raisins is slightly different from that used for coating creams. Secure Sultana raisins and wash and steam them. Melt sweet chocolate to 80 degrees and into it pour the raisins. Mix thoroughly and then dip out in spoonfuls on waxed paper. Equal quantities of raisins and chocolate make just about the right proportion for this confection.

Materials for Samplers

We are able to supply students with materials for samplers at the following prices: For Essential Stitches and Seams, Part 1, 25 cents; for Part 2, 50 cents; for Millinery Stitches, 40 cents; for Embroidery Stitches, Parts 1 and 2, 25 cents.

New students especially may be glad to take advantage of these materials, as they are well worth the price.

Students, of course, may use materials they have on hand for making samplers. They may even substitute if they do not have the exact materials asked for in the lessons, but in such cases they should call our attention to the fact by pinning a note to the sampler.

News About Our Testimonial

By JANE THOMAS
Membership Secretary

WHEN this copy of INSPIRATION reaches you, there will be only a very few days remaining in our Testimonial to Mrs. Picken. But they will be very important days, for they will be days during which those members who have not as yet been able to take part in this Testimonial to Mrs. Picken will have their last opportunity to get the one new member that will give them this honor. And what a wonderful Testimonial it has been—a Testimonial perfectly in keeping with the great work Mrs. Picken is doing for women—a Testimonial that is a monument in itself to the gratitude and appreciation of the great body of fine women who make up our membership.

INDEED, the response of our members has exceeded our most extravagant expectations, so that we are now ambitious that every active member enjoy the honor of having a part in this fine Testimonial. What a wonderful thing it would be, at our Fourth Anniversary observance when we present Mrs. Picken with the handsome brochure of those who got at least one new member during the Testimonial, if this brochure could contain the name of every active student in our membership. I am sure that every one of our members will want to enjoy that distinction, and it is not too late for any one to get the one new member necessary.

Perhaps you have been thinking about speaking to one or two of your friends but have not been able to do so—I know that you must be busy, for all of our members are busy women. These friends, even now, may be thinking about writing to the Institute. Doubtless they will join some time because women are more and more realizing the growing necessity of learning how to make their own clothes and hats. But I am anxious that they join now so you may have the credit for their enrolments. Won't you try to see them soon?

YOU will be interested, I am sure, in learning the name of the fortunate woman who won the handsome silk dress for January. This extreme good fortune, for certainly it is good fortune in these days of the high cost of clothes to get a beautiful silk dress with no expense whatever, went to Mrs. Elbert McCollum, of Simsbury, Connecticut. And Mrs. Picken is taking a great deal of pleasure in helping Mrs. McCollum to plan it and design it so as to get the most beautiful effect possible.

THEN I am sure that many of our members are thinking about the four free trips to Scranton and the Special Gifts that will be given to the members who give us the greatest amount of cooperation. We are planning to make our Fourth Anniversary Observance a fitting climax to our Testimonial to Mrs. Picken, as well as thoroughly in keeping with the wonderful progress that has been made by the Insti-

tute during the four years since the enrolment of our first student. We, here at headquarters, are looking forward with a great deal of pleasure to this event and to the privilege of meeting and entertaining some of our members. And I know that many of our members are anticipating with equally as much pleasure the prospect of being one of the women who will enjoy this event with us.

IN ADDITION to the four free trips to Scranton, the following Special Gifts will be awarded to those students who stand at the head of the list in the number of new members they help us to enroll: An $80 White Rotary Sewing Machine. A $65 Wilson Electric Portable Sewing Machine. A $60 Napanee Kitchen Cabinet. A Full-Paid Scholarship in any Woman's Institute Course. A $45 15-Jeweled Elgin Bracelet Watch. A $37.50 Set of Oneida Community Silverware. A $25 Solid Mahogany Martha Washington Sewing Companion. A $23 Seventeen-Section Hall-Borchert Adjustable Dress Form. A $15 Twelve-Section Hall-Borchert Adjustable Dress Form. A $14 Sanitary Kitchen Table with White Enamel Top.

AND I want to say again what I have already said several times—that everybody is going to be surprised when they learn what a small number of new students it was necessary to get in order to earn these Special Gifts.

I thoroughly believe there are very few of our members who could not, even now, get enough new students to win one of these Special Gifts. I cannot make this too strong, because if I can prevent it, I don't want any of our members to feel, after the Testimonial is over, that she might have earned one of the trips to Scranton or one of these Special Gifts if she had only realized that it was going to be so easy.

I AM arranging to enclose an Application blank with this copy of INSPIRATION. And I suggest that during the next few days you visit the friends you have been thinking about speaking to, and tell them just what the Institute is doing for you. Show them one of your Instruction Papers, preferably one of the more elementary ones, and also one of your corrected lessons, which

will show how carefully and thoroughly we inspect and correct your work. You will find the prices of the Courses very plainly printed on the Application and you may tell your friend that if she joins now we will give her the Dress Form or the Millinery or Cooking Outfit free of cost. Have her fill in the Application and hand you her remittance for the amount she wishes to pay down. You may then send the Application and remittance to us and we will see that the enrolment is placed to your credit.

TO THOSE members who have sent us names of friends who have not as yet joined I want to give a few words in closing. The contest for the trips to Scranton and the Special Gifts is very close. Not any one student has developed any lead over the others. In fact, as I write this article, four are tie for first place and there are scores of others so close that a single enrolment will change their standing. It is absolutely impossible even to hazard a guess as to who might be among the winners. So close are the contestants that it is possible for some of the hundreds of students with only one new student to their credit to jump into the lead at any time.

WE HAVE written to the women whose names you have sent us. But there may be some little point about which they are in doubt and which you could easily clear up for them. Won't you, during the next few days, arrange to see each of the women whose names you sent us? No doubt you can give them any information they may wish and help them to decide to join now. Show them how to fill out their Application Blank, get their remittance for their first payment, and then send their Application and remittance along to us, and it will count to your credit in the Testimonial. Perhaps this will be the one enrolment you will need to win the trip to Scranton or one of the Special Gifts.

Fashion Service

SUPPLEMENT

Each Issue of *Vintage Notions Monthly* includes a *Fashion Service Supplement*. You will read about the fashion styles popular in the early twentieth century and receive a collectible fashion illustration to print and frame.

The students of the Woman's Institute would also receive a publication called *Fashion Service*. Where the *Inspiration* newsletter instructed them on all aspects of the domestic arts, not only sewing but also cooking, housekeeping, decorating, etc., *Fashion Service* was devoted entirely to giving current fashions with a key to their development.

Fashion Service prided itself on providing it's readers with reliable style information and the newest fashion forecasting. The publication wasn't just eye candy. The Institute stressed the importance of studying the fashions to benefit the sewer's understanding of dressmaking. To quote founder Mary Brooks Picken, "Once the principles of design...and of construction… are understood, beautiful garments will result. This publication comes to you as an aid to this desired goal. Read the text of every page and reason out the why of every illustration and description that your comprehension of designing and construction may be enlarged and your appreciation made more acute."

Today, these articles and illustrations give us a historically accurate view of what fashion really meant 100 years ago. Not only can we study these articles for an "of-the-time" style snapshot, but just as their students did, we can also learn to understand the principles of design and increase our sewing skills. In each issue, look for a collectible illustration in the back of the supplement!

Tuxedo-Scarf Dress

Style.—The Tuxedo-scarf effect is a modification of the Tuxedo revers, which has become a factor in smart clothes. Coats, dresses, and evening gowns carry the Tuxedo line with success. It has many virtues in that it can be arranged to increase or decrease the width across the front, and especially through the shoulders, the slight figure using a more generous scarf effect than would be becoming to a stout figure.

Kimono or set-in sleeves may be used for this model. When a kimono sleeve is used, a loose panel of the kind illustrated is a commendable feature. Some backs are greatly improved by panels, while erect figures with thin shoulders may use the kimono without the panel with good success. Others should provide panels whenever possible.

The kimono type of sleeve should be carefully considered for becomingness and need. Such sleeves fitted as close as are smart this season are rarely comfortable when long. The short or three-quarter sleeves call for long gloves, and long gloves of right color are the very essence of smartness just now.

Material and Pattern.—Silk materials, such as satin, crêpe de Chine, crêpe de meteor, and the novelty weaves of very fine texture are suitable for a dress of this style. As a pronounced vogue of satin is now prevalent, this was chosen in a popular brown, tete de negre, for this particular style. The trimming is of an unusual nature, both as to the kind, it being loop fringe, and the manner in which it is employed to form rosettes. Fringe of this kind consists of a series of loops made of heavy silk floss and held into a narrow, firm edge. Fine grosgrain ribbon may be substituted for fringe, if desired. The vestee and the trimming band that extends below the waist line are of tan Georgette embroidered with beads.

For cutting this dress for the average figure, 5 yards of satin, ⅜ yard of Georgette crêpe, and 10 or 11 yards of fringe are necessary. For a waist lining 1 yard of soft silk or, if preferred, light-weight lawn should be provided. A waist lining is almost a necessity in any dress that may not be laundered, for even though such a lining is not required for a foundation, it serves as a protection to the dress and prevents it from becoming soiled or worn too readily. If the lining is merely tacked in position, it may be easily removed from the dress so that it may be laundered frequently.

A special pattern does not necessarily have to be purchased for this style, as its features are very simple and may be easily developed. A plain-waist pattern, having either kimono or separate sleeves should be used as a foundation. Mark on this the vest line and also the back-panel section, provided a kimono foundation is employed. Then, to form the pattern for the tuxedo-scarf effect, experiment with muslin. Pin a lengthwise thread of this at the center-back neck line of the form, draw the material around toward the front, making it assume the roll that is desired, and turn under the edges to form a scarf effect that is becoming in regard to width. Finally, cut the outside and neck edges of the model to produce just the effect you desire. Form the cuff pattern from paper or muslin.

Cutting.—First cut two straight lengths of material for the skirt, making each of these about 27 inches wide and the desired skirt length, plus allowance for the tucks and hem. For instance, if you desire tucks 3 inches wide, it will be necessary for you to allow 12 inches on each skirt length for tucks; that is, 6 inches for each tuck. It is advisable to draw a thread when cutting straight lengths of material, for this insures accurate results that are difficult to obtain otherwise. Most of the straight skirts have hems about 3½ to 6 inches deep this season. At this time decide just where the tucks should be placed in the skirt to make it most becoming.

Place the collar pattern so that the front line comes on a lengthwise thread with a bias seam at the center back. Lay the center back of the panel portion on a lengthwise fold and the side section of the waist pattern so that a lengthwise thread will extend from the neck end of the shoulder on a straight line to the waist line. This will make necessary a slightly bias seam at the back. Place the center of the cuff pattern on a lengthwise thread, and in cutting provide for double cuffs.

For the belt, cut a bias strip of material about 6 inches wide and several inches longer than the waist measurement, and for the sash ends cut double strips of the same width and about 18 inches long. Cut the Georgette vest single, but cut the trimming band double so that it will be, when finished, a straight piece about 10 inches wide and 4 inches long.

Construction.—Join the skirt gores with plain pressed-open seams, leaving the left one open at the top for a placket, and then baste the hem and tucks in position. Next, measure the correct front, side, and back skirt lengths from the lower edge of the hem, connect these points with a gradual curved line, and follow this line in running the gathering thread. A straight gathered skirt having tucks can generally be hung satisfactorily from the waist line, for if it is measured carefully, the length requires but little adjustment. Baste the center-back and under-arm seams of the waist.

Fitting.—Fit the lining first; then, the kimono waist, noting especially the under arm. If it appears too baggy here, pin the seam a trifle deeper. If this does not seem to remedy the difficulty, remove the basting at the under arm and, if necessary, in the sleeve seam; also, you may find it advisable to take in the front of the seam a trifle more than the back in order to make the waist fit properly. Pin the back panel in position and turn under the edges to make it of a becoming width. Pin the fulness at the lower edge of the waist to an inside stay belt arranged to have the opening at the center front. Then pin the skirt to the belting, keeping in mind the fact that the waist and the skirt must be finished separately at the waist line from the center front to the left side seam, for the skirt placket is arranged at this point.

Finishing.—Join the under arms with a plain pressed-open seam, and clip this at the under-arm curve. If you are using heavy material, it will be advisable to stay the under arm in the manner directed in your lessons. Face the back-panel edges and secure the panel at the neck and waist line. Then, in order to produce the soft effect so popular this season, secure the skirt tucks with fine running-stitches.

Next, make the collar, cuffs, and girdle. Make the cuffs double and slip-stitch the fringe in position, so that its finished edge is concealed just under the cuff edge. Face the collar with a very narrow bias strip and secure the inner edge with rather loose hemming-stitches that are barely discernible on the right side. Finish the girdle in the same manner, and apply the fringe to these pieces and also to the skirt tucks in the way in which it is secured to the cuffs. Make the girdle ends by folding the strips lengthwise through the center, right sides together, and stitching along the edge and one end. Then turn the strips right side out.

Make the fringe rosettes on a foundation of soft taffeta. Start arranging the fringe at the outside of the circle, which may be picot-edged, and lay and tack it in circular rows, each row just overlapping the preceding one, until the center is reached. Finish the center by tucking the end of the fringe under.

Bead the vest and trimming band. Slip the dress on and pin these sections, as well as the collar, cuffs, girdle, and rosettes, in position. Tack the girdle and rosettes carefully in place, so that they will not appear stiff; also, apply any other necessary finishing details.

Look for a collectible print version at the end of this issue.

Model 2

Variations of Tuxedo-Scarf Dress

Model 2A.—Chiffon velvet, because of its richness and deep color tone, is sufficient in itself to excite admiration, but when, in a model such as this, it assumes rust color and chooses to combine with an excellent quality of the same color satin and uses fur and metallic embroidery for trimming, it seems to have reached the very height of perfection. The long front panel, which is looped under the skirt hem, the shape of the cuffs and the narrow fur collar, and the arrangement of the girdle ends make the style suitable for medium-stout figures.

For the average figure, 2¾ yards of velvet and 1⅛ yards of satin are required; 3⅓ yards of narrow fur is sufficient for trimming the dress as illustrated. A strip of inexpensive silk or lining material about 1⅛ yards long should also be provided for the foundation under the satin panel.

Before cutting the material, plan the panel width in order to make it as becoming as possible. In this case, the panel width was made about 20 inches and was cut straight without goring and about 1 inch longer than the skirt length was cut. Make the remainder of the skirt of one full width of velvet, provided this is 40 inches wide, and attach this to a front panel 8 to 10 inches wide cut of the lining material. Either hem or picot the outer satin panel edges; then secure this panel to the center-front waist line of the skirt, and loop the other end under the lower edge and secure it with the hem. Face the girdle ends of velvet with satin or Georgette crêpe of a matching color and face the neck line of the dress before applying the fur.

Model 2B.—Too much cannot be said in regard to lace, for its present vogue surpasses in popularity and varied uses any attention that has been given to it for many years. Laces are used not only for trimming and for the development of entire dresses, but also for developing capes and wraps.

Fine vals, torchons, and Chantilly in lace, insertion, and flouncings find ready favor and are all that one could desire in regard to beauty. An especially smart combination is black lace with black satin, as in this dress. A touch of color, as well as a very appropriate finish for the lace, is provided in the binding of narrow greenish-blue ribbon used to edge the scarf effect, the inserted portion in the sleeve, and the band in the skirt. The sash end is finished with blue and black beads. Provide 3½ yards of satin, 3 yards of insertion about 7 inches wide, and 5 yards of ribbon for the average figure.

Make the scarf effect of a straight strip of insertion and dart it in at the back neck line to make it roll and fit properly. In cutting the scarf effect, extend it below the waist line to make it of a becoming length. Cut the sleeve rather wide through the lower portion, slash it at the point indicated, and let the back edge of the slash extend in a decided point about 2 inches below the front. Then face this point as well as the lower edge of the sleeve, insert the strip of lace, and turn the pointed portion of the sleeve back under the lace to produce the effect illustrated. Because of the open texture of the lace band, a black underskirt of soft silk should be provided for this dress.

Model 2C.—As a rule, elaborateness of design is quite out of place in a dress of striking color. This accounts for the simplicity of the design chosen for American Beauty satin and matching chiffon. Interest, other than that provided in the color, is afforded by the bead embroidery and the attractive arrangement of flowers at the waist-line closing. Another possibility of this design is brown satin and ecru chiffon embroidered with bronze beads.

For the average figure, 4 yards of satin and 1⅛ yards of chiffon will suffice. In cutting, arrange for an entire skirt of satin with the tucks running under the loose panel of chiffon. Provide a surplice extension for the scarf effect, and cut the scarf so that its outside edges are on a lengthwise thread. This will cause a bias seam at the center back which should be finished with machine hemstitching and trimmed close to make it as flat as possible. Finish the outer edge of the collar and the sides of the skirt panel with picoting, and turn a hem in the lower edge of the panel, which, together with the beads, will prevent the panel from curling up.

Model 2D.—In this design, cocoa-brown satin is very pleasingly set off by facings of velvet in Capri blue, which is a medium shade having an ever so slight suggestion of green. The vestee is of brown indestructible voile with embroidery in heavy silk floss, which again appears near the lower edge of the skirt. The material requirements of this model are 5 yards of satin, ½ yard of indestructible voile, 1 yard of velvet, and ¾ yard of lining for the upper back portion of the underskirt.

To arrange for the drop shoulder, mark this on the kimono pattern, and to provide fulness in the lower edge of the sleeve, slash and separate the lower sleeve portion when cutting the material. In making the sleeve, slash it diagonally about 3½ inches in front of the seam and conceal one end of the straight trimming band in the dart thus formed, as the illustration shows, and the other end in the sleeve seam. Face the inside of this band with velvet.

Outline a straight overskirt with its yoke section on a plain-skirt pattern. Then, in cutting, slash and separate the yoke sections to provide just a little fulness; also, slash and separate the lower part to make its lines practically straight and provide considerable fulness to be gathered into the yoke section. Join the overskirt and yoke sections by means of a very narrow tucked seam, making the overskirt appear as if set on to the yoke. To form the pointed effect, piece the lower front edge of the overskirt just under the looped portion.

Cut the velvet facings straight of the material, having them about 9 inches wide at the lower edge and tapering them to a width of 2 or 3 inches near the waist line. Do not attempt to secure the inner edge of the facing to the overskirt, for this would produce a rather stiff, conspicuous finish. Merely overcast or bind the edge of the velvet and leave this free. Then gather the lower edge of the overskirt and secure this to the underskirt to produce a puffed or harem effect.

Model 2E.—When one's allegiance holds steadfastly to blue, what is better than varying materials and thus adding variety to one's wardrobe? Velvet is the logical choice when an elegant costume is desired, and if, in addition, a digression from blue is permitted in a full-length front-panel effect of gray indestructible voile, one has a costume that far surpasses almost any other in one's wardrobe.

A dress is hardly complete this season without a touch of embroidery or a few dangling beads. Therefore, with very good reason, embroidery of heavy blue-silk floss and silver thread is used near the waist line of the panel and to emphasize the hip line, and blue and silver beads finish the panel at its lower edge. The silver cord used at the waist line is a favored example of the very narrow girdle finishes.

For the average figure, provide 2¼ yards of velvet and 1½ yards of indestructible voile. Cut the front skirt panel from 13 to 18 inches wide, depending on the figure. Form the remainder of the skirt of one straight length of velvet. In joining the velvet and voile, stitch them in a narrow plain seam; then turn the velvet back so that it extends about 1 inch over the voile, and secure the plain seam to the velvet by means of loose catch-stitches.

For the circular cuff, outline a straight cuff on the sleeve pattern; then slash the cuff pattern in several places from the lower edge almost to the top and separate to provide just the flare you desire. Line the cuffs with indestructible voile.

For wear under this dress, provide a slip of China silk in a rather bright blue. This will make unnecessary the wearing of an underskirt and also prove an attractive finish under the gray.

2A

2B

2C

2E

2D

Long-Waisted Dress

Style.—The Moyen-âge, or long-waisted, dress occupies a very definite place in the fashions of fall and winter. Slenderness and simplicity, which tend to youthfulness and dignity, are the most characteristic features. Such a dress is becoming to tall and medium-tall figures who are not definitely large through the bust or the hips. For figures with proportionately large bust and hips, unless the hem of the tunic is heavily weighted, the garment would have a tendency to fall in at the waist line, thus interfering to a considerable degree with the smartness of the style.

Material and Pattern.—Cloth medium light in weight, satin, Canton crêpe, and faille are excellent for this type of dress, for it requires a material luxuriously soft and yet with enough body to hold in shape.

For the average figure, 3¾ yards of 54-inch cloth or 4½ to 5 yards of 40-inch satin will be the right amount for such a dress, with ½ yard of material for trimming and 1 yard of 36-inch material for lining.

Pictorial Review design No. 9071 carries the foundation pattern lines that make possible the development of long-waisted dresses. Study the illustration closely and adjust the pattern to conform to the lines that you know to be most becoming and satisfactory to you. Determine upon the length of the waist, whether you will use darts to the bust points or seams from the shoulders to the bottom of the waist, and whether the closing will be at the center front, the center back, or the side. Also, determine whether you will use a plain, an accordion-plaited, a tunic, or a harem skirt. By carefully determining these matters, you will be able to produce a more satisfactory and individually becoming garment than if you cut your material at random with the thought of making the necessary adjustments in the fitting. In addition, you will prevent its acquiring an amateurish or home-made look.

Cutting.—To cut out this dress, which is made of blue tricotine, first, for the vest effect, fold back the front of the waist pattern and mark and cut the side-front and side-back seam lines. Then place the vest edge of the front on a lengthwise thread, the center back on a lengthwise fold, and the side-front and side-back sections so that the lengthwise center of each is on a lengthwise thread of the material.

For the plaited tunic, cut three straight pieces of material of a length you consider suitable for your type. This season a generous seven-eighths of the finished skirt length is employed. Make one of these pieces of a width equal to the distance at the lower edge of the waist from one side-back seam to the other, plus allowance for plaits on each edge. Make the other two pieces of a width equal to the distance from the vest line to the side-back seam, plus allowance for the number of plaits desired, remembering that each plait requires three times its depth.

For the belt, provide a lengthwise strip of material about 3 inches wide and 2 yards long, planning as few piecings in this as necessary. Cut the cuffs and vest from straight pieces of the trimming material, which is tan duvetyn, and form the collar pattern by experimenting with muslin. Cut the waist lining or underbody in the usual manner.

Fitting.—In preparing for the fitting, place a facing of the dress material about 3 inches deep around the armhole of the waist lining, and then baste the lining seams and run a gathering thread at the waist line. As the foundation skirt may be gathered at the waist line or fitted by means of darts, the skirt seams may be finished with a plain pressed-open seam before the first fitting. Leave the upper part of the left seam open and finish this with a continuous or flat-stitched continuous placket. Then gather or lay darts in the upper edge of the skirt.

Join the overskirt sections by means of plain pressed-open seams. Baste the plaits in position. Then baste the waist seams, turn under the lower edge of the waist, and baste this to the tunic, following the general directions already studied in doing all this work.

Next, hook in position on the figure a piece of inside stay belting prepared according to instructions given in your lessons. The belting should be cut long enough to prevent a tight waist-line effect, and just loose enough to accord with the straight silhouette. Place the waist lining on the figure, do any fitting that may be necessary, and pin the lining to the belt, adjusting the fulness properly. At this time, also, pin the sleeves in position. Then bring the waist line of the foundation skirt over the lower edge of the waist and pin this to the inside stay belting, arranging the fulness so that the skirt sits properly. Stay the fulness of the front gore from the center front to the left side seam with a piece of tape, in order to prepare for the closing.

Slip on the overdress and note the points generally observed in fitting, as described in your lessons. A very important detail in the fitting of a dress of this kind is the effect at the back neck line and shoulder seams. If, after the dress has been on the figure a few minutes, it has a tendency to fall away from the neck line at the back, remove the shoulder bastings and lift the back portion of the waist a trifle. Then pin the new shoulder line and reshape the neck line if necessary. Turn the lower edge of the overskirt the desired length; also, turn the hem in the foundation skirt.

Construction.—Proceed with the making of the dress by finishing the seams, the neck, the front edges of the lining, and the waist-line closing of the skirt, and apply snap fasteners the entire length of the foundation closing. Attach the sleeves to the lining by means of plain seams. Then press the seam edges together so that they turn toward the waist rather than out into the sleeve. Face the lower edge of the sleeves with light-weight silk. Remove the tunic from the waist and finish the side waist seams as single-stitched seams, making the stitching a scant ⅛ inch from the seam line.

Make plain pressed-open seams at the shoulder and under arm. Hem the sides and lower edge of the tunic with fine but rather loose stitches, and press the plaits in position. Then baste the tunic to the lower edge of the waist.

Fold the strip for the girdle lengthwise through the center and stitch a plain seam. Then turn the girdle right side out so that the raw edges are concealed. Next, prepare the collar, cuffs, and vest. For the trimming that is illustrated, ⅛ yard of blue suède is required. Cut the suède motifs of the desired size and shape. Plan their arrangement and then appliqué them to the duvetyn by means of chain-stitching or blanket-stitching. Face the upper and lower edges of the vest section, and line the cuffs with satin or soft silk of a matching color. Line the collar with material like that used for the dress.

With the dress in this condition, slip it on the figure. Pin the vest, collar, cuffs, and girdle in position and make any slight changes that you may consider advisable in order to add to the becomingness of this style.

Finishing.—Stitch the waist to the tunic to make the finish correspond with that used in the side waist seams. Then overcast the raw edges or bind them with silk seam binding. Secure the front edges of the waist with fine hemming-stitches, taking care not to have them show on the right side. Bind the lengthwise edges of the vest, tack this in position, cover the joining of the collar with a narrow bias strip of silk, and secure the cuffs in position by means of slip-stitching.

Then sew on the buttons and apply snap fasteners to the side front overdress closing. Secure weights in the hem of the tunic near the front edges, and then press the dress carefully.

Model 3

Variations of Long-Waisted Dress

Model 3A.—Model 3A, which is a slip-over style that would serve for street or afternoon wear, is a rather simple although quite distinctive variation of the long-waisted dress. Not only has it drawn from one of the most popular of the fall fabrics, black satin, but also has it selected duvetyn in that very new blue, radio by name, for its odd trimming bands. Then, to make these bands of further interest, it has added silver embroidery. The harem skirt is another good style feature in this design, for the puffed effect serves to bring out the sheen and beauty of texture of the satin. However, a harem skirt is not attractive if the finished width is more than 1½ yards, and naturally such a skirt will have a tendency to creep up a certain extent when worn. Therefore, it is not especially desirable for stout or matronly figures.

The development of this dress, for the average figure, requires 3¾ yards of satin and ⅜ yard of duvetyn, with 2 yards of light-weight silk or lining for the foundation skirt.

The harem skirt should be cut straight and about 2 yards wide and several inches longer than the desired skirt length. The foundation should be no more than 1½ yards wide. To produce the harem effect, gather the outer skirt at the lower edge, bring this up inside of the turned lower edge of the foundation skirt and slip-stitch this in position.

Cut the sleeve three-quarter length, face the lower edge, leave the lower end of the seam free, and turn back and tack the corners to produce the effect illustrated. Face the neck and the slashed opening in the waist.

Six pieces of duvetyn, 6 inches by 10 inches, are picoted on their four sides and then embroidered and placed as illustrated for decoration on the skirt and at the waist line. Very small figures will need to decrease the size of these pieces, and larger figures to increase them slightly to have them in right proportion.

Model 3B.—Chinchilla satin in autumn brown shows its partiality to self-toned trimming by its unusual use of pheasant-colored embroidery. An extension on the wide back skirt panel is caught up with a tassel at each side front in such a manner as to produce a slightly draped effect.

For the average figure, 4½ yards of satin is sufficient for this style. In cutting the back panel, make it the full skirt length and gore it a trifle, making it 30 to 32 inches at the waist line and about 4 inches wider at the lower edge. It is not necessary to shape the panel other than to gore it as suggested, for a piece cut in this manner can be tacked up at the front and made to assume the draped effect that is illustrated. Finish the edges of the panel with picoting.

To form the sleeve, cut it rather wide through the lower portion, slash it as illustrated, and extend the central part 7 or 8 inches beyond the desired finished length, making the extended portion about 4 inches wide. In making, picot the edges, turn the extended portion of the sleeve back on a diagonal line so that it fills in a part of the slashed portion, and hold this in position with the stitches that secure the buttons. Form the collar pattern by experimenting with muslin.

Model 3C.—Duvetyn, that soft, lovely woolen material which is receiving so much favor at present, chose dark blue as its color for this street dress. Then, as the high collar is the latest word in fashion, it added squirrel as a companion for the gray-looped fringe trimming and produced results quite out of the ordinary. A muff of squirrel to be carried with such a frock is an accessory worthy of note.

Provide 3½ yards of duvetyn and 7¼ yards of fringe for the average figure. Hem the outer edges of the tunic and miter the corners very carefully in order to make them appear true and well tailored. For the collar, provide a strip of fur that is long enough to be comfortable and yet will not make the collar so large that it detracts from a neat or well-fitted effect.

Finish the edges of the fur by binding them with a very narrow strip of silk or tape. Then apply a soft-silk lining to the collar, securing it to the binding by means of slip-stitches. Arrange the closing of the collar at the left side and that of the dress at the left shoulder and under arm.

Model 3D.—Threads of metallic luster predominate in the evidences of hand embroidery that are shown on fall dresses. In this particular model, gold embroidery is skilfully used to enhance further the appearance of a dress of snuff-brown satin, which alone is very interesting in design. Of all the variations of the long-waisted dress, this model is best suited to the matron.

For the average figure, 4½ to 5½ yards of 40-inch satin will prove ample for this style of dress. An unusual construction feature is brought into consideration by the side draperies. Make such a drapery of a true bias strip of material about 2¼ yards long and 9 inches wide at the ends and broadening to 14 to 16 inches through the center of the strip. Have the edges of this strip picoted, and secure the ends with the joining of the waist and skirt. Lay a few soft folds in the looped portion of the strip in order to make it assume the draped effect that is illustrated. Cut the three-quarter sleeves from 13 to 15 inches wide at the lower edge.

Model 3E.—Although a great many of the fall collections of evening gowns are rather severe, they suggest the very spirit of luxury, for almost invariably they are made of rich fabrics, and often the decoration is of a costly nature. This model of chiffon velvet in black, a great favorite for evening wear, is an example of a rather severe type of dress; but in this case the effect is softened by side draperies and tiny sleeves of black tulle. The embroidery consists of silver thread and spangles, an unusual and lovely combination, but, withal, a quite inexpensive decoration.

For this dress, 3¼ yards of chiffon velvet and 1¾ yards of tulle 36 inches wide are the material requirements. To form the side drapery, use a piece of tulle 18 inches wide and about 1½ yards long; tack one end underneath the hem of the skirt, bring the other end to the low waist line of the dress, and loop this down to form the bouffant effect.

If you wish to soften the neck line of the dress, you may edge it with a bias fold of tulle.

Model 3F.—For evening wear, if one has grown tired of the somber hues of street clothes in general, one may indulge freely in colors that are striking and strictly in accordance with one's love of beauty. And what could hold one's fancy better than this gown with a bodice of Adriatic-blue chiffon velvet, loose skirt panels of this same material accentuated by trimming of blue spangles and beads, a skirt of silver net and lace over blue-metal cloth, and a shower of silver net held at one shoulder with a rose that provides just the right color contrast? But if one's means are limited, one need not pass by this style, for it is suggestive of many possibilities in development. For instance, a combination of less expensive lace or tulle with satin would prove very attractive. The spangles and beads may be omitted with no ill effect.

The material requirements of this dress include 1½ yards of velvet, 1¾ yards of 36-inch tulle, 2 yards of lace skirting, 1½ yards of 36-inch metal cloth, and ½ yard of silk that matches the velvet and is used for facing the skirt panels. The metal cloth is seamed together crosswise and has but one seam. This seam and the placket opening are arranged to come under the strap at the left side.

In cutting the bodice, allow a little extra length, so that it may be crushed softly through the lower portion and a little fulness gathered in at the front under-arm seams. Plan the cutting so that six panels, each about 2½ inches wide, may be taken, without piecing, from one edge of the piece of velvet.

3A

3B

3E

3C

3D

3F

Kimono Waist-Line Dress

Style.—Kimono sleeves, because of their grace and adaptability to materials and fashions, frequently come definitely to the fore. Today they are seriously the vogue, and agreeably so because of the loose waist line with which they are used.

Slender figures can wear kimono-cut waists with a great deal of satisfaction. Even a heavy figure can wear them becomingly, provided a panel or a panel back is used to narrow in appearance the width of back and a vest effect or definite front and collar line is employed, the Tuxedo collar effect being frequently adaptable.

A recent cable from Paris gave this fashion information: "Panels back and front on waists; panels up and down on skirts; ribbons galore; hours of embroidery; much lace; some buttons; and every other blouse a kimono sleeve." Perhaps the model here shown is that message interpreted; at any rate, it is a delightful compromise.

Material and Pattern.—Satin, crêpe meteor, Canton crêpe, crêpe de Chine, and silk poplin used with Georgette are appropriate for this type of dress. For it 4½ to 5 yards of material, 1 yard of Georgette, 4½ yards of double-faced ribbon ⅜ to ⅞ inch wide, and 10 to 12 skeins of embroidery floss are needed.

The original dress was of dark-blue crêpe meteor, with henna Georgette collar, sleeves, and embroidery. Black satin with rust Georgette and embroidery and sparrow-colored satin with a lighter tan Georgette and brown embroidery are excellent color combinations. Then there is the silver-gray and light-yellow combination, the silver-gray and pale-rose combination, and the navy and deep blue-gray combination, any of which makes a good color effect, especially for a very dainty dress.

The Buster Brown or Dutch collar is always a favorite, and is to be seen this year on stately dinner gowns and on the plainest of dresses. It seems that it has as many variations in materials and color as it has uses. Exquisite laces, Georgettes, marquisettes, satins, brocaded ribbons, fur, and fur-cloth all lend themselves to this simplest of collars. The collar line illustrated here is precisely the new line for this collar, though it may be narrowed at the sides and slightly lowered at the front for the round-faced, short-necked person. When the collar is narrowed at the sides, a slight point at the center back will prove pleasing.

A plain, close-fitting kimono-waist pattern may be used as a guide pattern for the blouse, and a straight two-gored skirt pattern for the skirt. First, prepare a plain foundation lining of light-weight silk and arrange the opening at the left-side front, so that it will not be visible when the vest of Georgette is in place.

The color of the lining under the Georgette vest should be taken into consideration when the color combination of the dress is decided on, so that a pleasing color effect may be secured here. For instance, if the Georgette is dark blue, a robin's-egg blue or a gold color will be pretty under it; if silver gray, then pale rose; if brown, then gold or a light blue. In any event, this contrasting color should harmonize with the embroidery and ribbon trimming of the dress.

Embroidery Designs.—Do not consider embroidery difficult; today it may be produced easily and quickly. The chief requisites are artistic designs and color combinations. Dress decorations should rarely dominate the dress; rather, the material of the dress, in color and texture, should be subordinate to the individual, and the embroidery, in design and coloring, subordinate to the material. Patchy embroidery or that which evidences hours of labor is rarely beautiful as dress decoration. Rather, embroidery should blend into the material and style and be inconspicuously decorative; seldom should it be dominant in line or color.

Study the designs given in the Embroidery Fashion Books to be found at all pattern counters, or visit a fancy goods shop or an art shop to see their special transfer designs. Among these, you can find designs that will help you materially to develop your own plan of decoration. You may not want to use all of any one design, but you can use a part or fit the design together to agree with your special need. For instance, a woman whose skirt length is short should not select an embroidery design that extends the full length of her tunic; but she could use, perhaps, a portion of a design so as to have the embroidery come in the right position for her. This may be arranged by cutting away any unnecessary part of the design before the transfer is made to the material.

Ribbons for Trimming.—One would scarcely delight in an all-ribbon frock, although such frocks are seen and are frequently quite attractive, but to see the exquisite ribbons of every color, tone, and hue, of every width and design, makes one eager to use them. Ribbons were never more beautiful nor more wholly adaptable than now. They are used on cloth, velvet, lace, satin, and Georgette, apparently without discrimination, and every ribbon seems to know just where it belongs.

As soon as you decide on the color of your dress, make it a point to see the ribbons. You are sure to find the right ribbon in width, texture, and coloring to help you with the trimming.

Cutting.—Place the center-back line of the kimono pattern on the center fold of a full width of material. This will bring the dropped armhole and the vest or front edges of the blouse on the half-bias, giving lines that are very satisfactory if the material does not stretch very much.

In the event that such material as Georgette crêpe or crêpe de Chine, which will stretch when cut on the bias, is used, cut the back with the seam at the center back on a ⅞ bias grain and then cover the seam with a panel 2¾ to 7 inches wide, the width of the panel depending on the width and length of back of the individual and on the material used.

Construction.—Sew the skirt and tunic seams and press them open. If the material is heavy, use a picot or a bias-bound edge for the tunic. If it is medium light in weight, turn a hem 1⅛ to 1½ inches wide at the sides and 2 inches at the bottom and carefully slip-stitch these in place, taking care to use easy stitches and to press carefully from the wrong side and allowing the pressing to aid in holding the turned edges in place, thus making close, substantial stitches unnecessary. Remember that a dress can be oversewed and thereby lose its smartness. First, plan for effect; then substantiate this with good workmanship, which does not always mean close stitches.

Finish the vest edge of the overblouse to harmonize with the finish of the tunic and the lower edge of the sleeve by binding it and tacking the ribbon in place. Join the sleeve to the dropped armhole by stitching a plain seam about 1/16 inch outside of the marked seam line. Then turn both seam edges in toward the waist, and with the armhole edge of the overblouse rolled down over the sleeve just enough to cover the seam line, cut the seam edge of the overblouse to make it about ⅛ inch narrower than the sleeve seam. Then turn the sleeve edge over this and secure the turned edge to the overblouse with fine, loose hemming-stitches. These stitches should be taken very carefully so that they will be scarcely evident on the right side. Then stamp or mark the embroidery design on the material and do the embroidery in the colors selected. When this is completed, press it on a well-padded board from the wrong side, handling the iron deftly, so as to allow the pressing to improve the appearance of both the stitches and the design, rather than to make them appear flat and definitely applied.

Model 4

Variations of Kimono Waist-Line Dress

Model 4A.—An interesting type of dress is shown here, because through it one can actually visualize the evolution of a certain pattern. Practically ever since the permanency of the normal waist line, this type of dress has been favored. It is modified each season and swings itself into favor by some definite concessions to Fashion's whims. But it has not yet been greatly changed.

This year, this type of dress carries the kimono sleeve and a slightly longer tunic, and has the tucks lifted from the bottom of the tunic or a little below the middle to a point slightly above the hip line, this being done to emphasize the width through the hips. These are the only noticeable changes. The collar, vest, and waist-line finish and the general skirt effect remain practically the same as that of last year and the year before.

Any of the soft silks or wool challis are appropriate for this type of dress, crêpe de Chine or crêpe meteor in brown, blue, gray, soft green, or black proving especially desirable.

To develop such a dress, cut the waist over a foundation kimono-waist pattern, with the center back on the lengthwise fold and the vest material on a straight grain of cloth. Make a foundation two-piece skirt with seams at the sides, and develop the tunic with one and one-half widths of 40-inch material cut lengthwise and joined with only one seam at the left side. The tunic should come from 2 to 3 inches above the bottom of the skirt hem, and the tucks should begin at a similar position below the waist line—that is, from 2 to 3 inches below. The width of the tucks depends somewhat on the material; if it is heavy, a narrow tuck usually looks best.

A bias sash from 9 to 12 inches wide, with a loop at the left side over the seam, will prove attractive. Many such waist lines are trimmed with a sash of picot-edged grosgrain ribbon from 1 to 3 inches wide and finished with long streamer ends of ribbon 1 to 1⅜ inches wide hanging down the left side.

A straight piece of Georgette or lace 3¼ to 4½ inches wide and from ½ to ¾ yard long will be sufficient for this collar.

Model 4B.—A good type of dress, especially if developed in duvetyn or velvet, is here illustrated. It is also very attractive when made of serge or tricotine. The material requirements are 4½ yards of 56-inch material or 6 yards of 40-inch material, together with ⅝ yard of 18-inch vesting and ¼ yard of 40-inch ruffling.

In this case, cut a long muslin model from a plain kimono-waist pattern for the overdress. Use the foundation two-piece skirt and the plain foundation waist. Sew the skirt to the waist lining and thus have the overdress entirely separate. Press the edges and the hem of the overdress carefully, and hold them back with slip-stitches so that they will not be prominent when the embroidery stitches are in place. The embroidery design for such a dress should not be too definite and should be worked rather at random in order to avoid having the lines too precise.

Model 4C.—Made of velvet, duvetyn, or very heavy satin, Model 4C is smart and at the same time very pleasing. The deep, soft colors of cocoa brown, ensign blue, and black are especially desirable for such a dress. The buttons may be plain ones of self-material; they may be made of self-material and embroidered in contrasting color; or they may be covered with material to match the collar, cuffs, and waist-line trimming.

The foundation kimono waist having a straight grain at the center front and being slightly bias at the back and a two-piece foundation-skirt pattern are right for this type of dress. In this case, the under-arm and skirt seams are arranged in open slot-seam effect, a straight strip of material 2½ inches wide being used for the slot seams in the skirt and a true bias strip provided for those of the under arm.

Model 4D.—This attractive dress consists of a plain-kimono blouse and a three-gored skirt, a deep-fold tuck being used at the center front. The collar is cut on the lengthwise thread of the material, with a bias seam at the center back. An embroidered band 10½ inches deep, or a little more than one-fourth the skirt length, is set into the skirt, and a similar one, a little more than half the sleeve length, forms the main part of the sleeve.

If the dress is of cloth, the trimming bands may be of duvetyn; if it is of satin or silk, the bands may be of Georgette, marquisette, or novelty net.

Many figures with full or slightly plump shoulders and neck complain that a kimono waist is short for them at the back of the neck. If they draw it up to its proper place at the neck, diagonal wrinkles form from the neck at the center-back to the side seams. To overcome this, first adjust the waist correctly on the figure. Then prepare a piece of self-material like a stand for a tailored coat collar, cutting it 8 to 10 inches long and 2 inches wide. Fold it crosswise through the center. Keep one edge straight and cut the other edge so that it will measure 2 inches at the fold and taper out to nothing at the straight edge. Next fit this shaped edge to the neck line of the kimono blouse, placing the fold of the piece exactly at the center back. This will give a higher neck line at the back and produce a better fitting and more comfortable collar and at the same time overcome the formation of wrinkles.

Model 4E.—Here we have a type of dress that is always well liked because of its becomingness and usefulness. It is suitable both for a dinner dress and for semi-evening wear. In addition, it is easily and quickly made, and if well done it will be much appreciated and admired. For the average or the large figure, 7 yards of lace 18 inches wide will be required.

A lace dress is seldom as conspicuous as one of silk or satin and therefore may be worn more frequently than a dress of other materials. Like ostrich feathers, lace comes into its own periodically. Its beauty and adaptability and general becomingness should keep it ever in fashion, but while good lace is almost always beautiful and thoroughly appreciated, it seems that fashion insists that it be tucked away for a year and sometimes two at a time. However, this year, even the tiniest piece can be brought forth and used with genuine satisfaction, for both the importers and our own manufacturers at the very outset of the season made certain that laces should find a definite and prominent place in this season's wardrobe.

To develop a pattern for this model, use a foundation kimono blouse cut with the center back and center front on a lengthwise fold, just as if you were cutting a kimono night dress. Arrange the opening to come under the ribbon at the left side front.

Usually a foundation two-gored skirt for such a dress is made of the same material as the blouse, although the blouse may be of Georgette or marquisette and the skirt of satin. Cut the skirt so that it is slightly narrow at its lower edge. This narrowness will necessitate 1 to 2½ inches additional length, for narrow skirts must of necessity be longer than full ones.

Join the foundation kimono waist and the skirt together, picoting or binding the neck edge and sleeves; then drape the lace as illustrated, taking care that just the right amount of fulness is provided.

Model 4F.—Overblouses are ever ready to lend themselves to new features in design, fabric, and trimming, and this versatility combined with their unrivaled usefulness has much to do with the favor that they seem so reluctant to forfeit. This is a particularly youthful model, both as to style and the fabric, which is Pussy-willow taffeta in amber color over a lining of very light ecru chiffon. The embroidery is of amber silk floss with greenish-blue beads providing an occasional touch of contrast.

4D

4E

4A

4C

4F

4B

Waist-Line Dress

Style.—A group of fashion women recently assembled were asked what type of dress they like best. They were equally divided between the one-piece and the waist-line dress. It would seem that the decision was made almost entirely from a personal point of view. Those women who required clothes for service and who had to be smartly dressed with very little time and effort selected the one-piece dress. Those whose clothes demands were not so serious chose the waist-line dress.

The dress featured here is in every way ideal for the dress-up dress, and it has also many possibilities for service. It is a practical dress, especially where few dresses can be had, because the drape may be easily changed to conform to any fashion. In addition, it is simple in line and consequently will stand considerable wear and yet hold its shape longer than some other types.

One may feel very safe in selecting this type of dress for continued wear, for dresses cut with the aid of a plain-waist pattern with panel-effect back and front and joined to a simple straight skirt are accepted each season, provided the waist line expresses newness in position and finish. Waist lines, for individual becomingness, should be tried out in front of the mirror with as much patience as is required in arranging a new coiffure.

Material and Pattern.—The model illustrated has a skirt of very dark-blue crêpe meteor and, over a gray Georgette foundation, a blouse of dark-blue Georgette, with a back panel of crêpe meteor. Gray, dull-silver, and American Beauty colored threads form the embroidery. The design is worked heavy across the front just above the waist, and then, in order to produce proper balance, is made lighter both in design and in color as it nears the shoulders. For the average figure, 4 yards of crêpe meteor, 1¾ yards of blue Georgette, and 1 yard of gray Georette should be provided.

A plain waist and a two-piece straight-skirt pattern are needed for the foundation. Try out in muslin at least the front and back waist panels in order to ascertain exactly their correct width and shaping. Cut the back panel from 4 to 6 inches longer than the back length, so that the upper end may be turned back 2 or 3 inches to form a fold or collar that will extend across the shoulders. Cut the foundation waist of gray Georgette and the back panel of crêpe meteor, allowing for a 1-inch hem on the lengthwise edges of the panel and a 2- or 3-inch hem at the top. Cut the front waist panel in one with the under-arm sections and provide for a plait about 1 inch wide to form this panel. For the skirt draperies, provide a 1¾-yard length of crêpe meteor cut the full width of the material.

Construction.—Baste the plaits to form the front panel of the waist. Then, with the foundation and outer waists together, baste the right-shoulder seam and both under-arm seams; also, baste the sleeve seams and the hems in the lengthwise and upper edges of the back panel. Next, slip on the waist so as to make sure that it fits correctly, and, in order to provide an opening, slash the left side of the waist and of the foundation at the inside edge of the tuck. Then pin the shoulder seam from the opening to the armhole edge. Also, mark the line for picoting the neck line of both the foundation and outer waists, arranging for the neck line of the foundation to extend above the neck line of the outer waist.

Remove the waist and have the neck edges picoted. At this time, also, have a row of hemstitching run through the lengthwise center and along one end of the piece cut for the draperies, and cut this through the hemstitched line to form a picoted edge for the upper part of each draped portion.

Before finishing the waist seams, apply the embroidery to the outer waist portion only. This will produce a softer finish than to take the embroidery stitches through the foundation after these parts are secured together. Then French-seam the shoulder and under-arm seams of the waist; also, join the sleeves and insert them with French seams. Bind the lengthwise edges of the opening with self-colored Georgette, and face both sides of the shoulder opening, making it as neat and inconspicuous as possible. Secure the hems in the back waist panel with fine, loose hemming-stitches.

Make plain pressed-open seams in the foundation skirt, but leave the left seam open at the top and finish it with a continuous placket. Then gather the waist line of the skirt.

With the parts of the dress thus prepared, placed them on the form, adjust the waist and skirt fulness to an inside stay belt, and turn the hem at the lower edge of the skirt.

Stay belts for this season are merely perfunctory in point of service because of the looseness of the waist line. Now they should be 1 to 3 inches larger than the waist measurement and in the majority of cases narrow. Frequently the 2½-inch belting is split through the center and bound on one edge with ribbon or silk seam binding, thus making one belt length serve for two dresses. A piece of the lining silk finished with a picoted edge or narrow lace makes a good covering for the belt. This piece of silk should be applied when the dress is practically complete.

To arrange the drapery for each side, secure, at the side front of the skirt, the unfinished end of one of the pieces that have been picoted. Arrange to have the selvage in the lower part of the drape and the picoted finish for the upper edge. Lay the fulness in soft plaits, arranging these to occupy a space of about 5 inches on each side. With this done, loop the material down at the side; then tack the upper finished corner at the side-back waist line, as the illustration shows.

Gauge the width between the drapes by the appearance of the individual. For large figures, bring the drapes closer together in order to form a narrower panel than is becoming to figures that are slighter. Soft plaits and drapes are very effective in satin and soft, luxurious materials, especially when designed to accord with the individual. Some designers contend that no rule can apply for drapery, for every dress has its own demands in this regard.

In order to prevent bulkiness in the drapery and to make it very soft and pretty, pin a dart from the upper edge of the center of the looped-down portion. Take up 10 to 12 inches in this dart and taper it so that it terminates about 4 inches above the selvage edge or just inside of the lowest fold of the drape. Stitch the dart in a plain seam and press this open to make it very flat. Then lay the looped portion in folds, extending these from the plaits at the waist line.

Finishing.—If the crêpe meteor or satin is heavy, the drapes will hold in place very nicely. If any difficulty is experienced, however, because the material is too light, sew a small weight at each inside fold so that the drapes will hold in place and the effect shown acquired.

Tack the back panel in position to produce the neck-line effect you desire. This will provide a fold to simulate a collar that extends straight across the back. The fold may be tacked merely at the shoulders and brought up high at the center back to stand up straight, or, if desired, it may be arranged so that it will flare out from the neck.

Make the girdle of a true-bias piece of crêpe meteor 11 inches wide, finishing the sides with a ⅝-inch hem slip-stitched in position. Gather the ends into the width desired when the girdle is crushed into position, and secure these gathered or shirred ends to a tape or light-weight covered bone. Then, to hold the girdle together securely, finish it with hooks and eyes.

Model 6

Variations of Waist-Line Dress

Model 6A.—A type of dress that really achieves slenderness in effect is shown in this model. The panels of the skirt, the long surplice waist, the long under-arm line, the close sleeve, and the high collar, all combine to evidence slenderness. In addition to these virtues, this dress offers excellent opportunities for remodeling because of the use of two materials, such as serge and satin, or broadcloth and satin.

The original of this dress is of black velvet combined with black-and-gold metal cloth. A self-covered button finishes the waist line closing at the under arm, and from this a black silk tassel is suspended. For the average figure, 2 yards of velvet and 1¾ yards of metal cloth 36 inches wide are required. For the Robespierre collar of fine silk-muslin or chiffon, provided this is desired, ½ yard of 18-inch material is required.

Develop the skirt and the waist from the plain foundation patterns. Cut and fit the overblouse in muslin to insure just the right length, width, and position, especially for the surplice effect and for the round flat collar, which extends across the back panel of velvet and covers the shoulder seam that joins this to the front surplice of metal cloth. Also, try out the Robespierre collar in lawn or cambric in order to procure just the right size, shape, and flare to make it individually becoming.

Make the opening of the dress at the left side front under the velvet panel, but extend the surplice to the left edge of the panel in the back so as to cover the end of the crushed girdle of metallic cloth that is placed across the back panel of velvet.

Model 6B.—Navy satin is combined with henna Georgette embroidered in silver for the dress shown in Model 6B. A tiny ribbon sash, ⅝ inch wide, of henna and silver is used as a waist-line finish, tying with a small bow at the center back. This dress gives opportunity for many pleasing color combinations. For instance, some very good ones are: gray and deep rose with old-blue embroidery; black and bright orchid with silver embroidery; black and white with gold embroidery; brown and tan with brown or gold embroidery.

Material requirements for making this dress for the average figure are 3¼ yards of satin, 1¼ yards of Georgette, and 2 yards of China silk for the upper part of the drop skirt.

Use a foundation-waist pattern for the blouse and the lining, and face the armholes of the satin with a ½-inch fitted strip, and those of the lining with a fitted piece of satin 2 inches wide. This finish will prevent the lining from showing when the Georgette sleeves are secured in position. For the collar, cut a 3-inch strip of Georgette, finish the outer edge with a ¼-inch finished Georgette binding, and embroider it in silver.

For cutting both the drop skirt and the tunic, use a plain straight-skirt pattern. Cut the upper part of the drop skirt of China or light-weight silk, and finish the lower edge with an 8- or 10-inch band of Georgette. Embroider 2 or 3 inches of this around the bottom. Make the width of the drop skirt at its lower edge but ⅓ yard less than the tunic. Because of the difference in color, only a slight difference is required in width between the tunic and the underskirt. Use a tiny cord in the curved tuck of the skirt to give a yoke effect across the front and sides, thus relieving the severe plainness. Form the back of the skirt of a straight, easy panel; that is, one that is slightly gathered into position.

Model 6C.—Good lines are evident throughout this model, which illustrates in a delightful way the emphasized straight silhouette that is just approaching. Some indefinite whispers from Europe are to the effect that the greyhound silhouette is near; but it is not yet definitely to be reckoned with and will not be as long as the kimono and tunic lines hold sway. Should greyhound lines assert themselves definitely, one would have to take a strip out of the skirt and add it to the length in order to be in keeping with the fashion; but this is hardly probable.

The opportunities for unusualness in color effect are excellent in Model 6C, which is so splendidly smart for a slender, lithesome figure. For instance, Moccasin brown with trimming of pheasant and a sash of pheasant-and-brown plaid, or even of bright gold-and-brown plaid, would indeed be unusual and pretty. The combination of blue serge with trimmings of Carnelian red, which, as you know, is a deep, rich American Beauty color, and a Carnelian and dark-blue sash would also prove striking in effect and yet appropriate and pleasing.

The sleeve of this model is interesting because of the slash, which discloses the facing of contrasting color, and the arrangement of the ribbon trimming above the slash. Sleeves, in general, show marked diversity in regard to length and style. The extremely short sleeve is not shown as frequently as it was several months ago, although it is evident in some models for afternoon or dinner wear. Silk dresses choose the elbow or three-quarter length type that is inclined to flare, or, in occasional instances, the long close-fitting variety, although this sleeve is generally used in tailored models. Evening dresses, in many cases, seem unaware of the existence of sleeves, but a short sleeve of sheer material that partly conceals the upper arm is always permissible and many times adds to the appearance of balance and completeness of the entire design.

This model requires 4 yards of 54-inch or 5 yards of 40-inch material, with ⅝ yard of silk for the girdle, sleeve facings, and vestee. For the trimming on the collar, vest, and sleeves, 3 yards of ½-inch ribbon is used, and 1½ to 1¾ yards of 1-inch ribbon is required for the panel of the skirt.

For the skirt, use two straight widths of 54-inch or two and one-half widths of 40-inch material. Make the front panel practically straight and 12 to 13 inches wide, or narrower if you consider it will be more becoming, and lay the knife plaits so as to meet at the center back. Cover the buttons neatly with self-material.

Model 6D.—Lace flouncing seems to find its most popular use in cascade draperies and surplice-waist effects, features that, while not startlingly new, are by no means ordinary, as this model will testify. Its skirt foundation is of black satin and its waist foundation of marquisette, although, if an extreme effect is desired, the waist foundation and the sleeves may be omitted and merely a straight bodice worn under the lace.

The material requirements for the average figure include 2¼ yards of satin, 4 yards of 14-inch flouncing, 1¼ yards of marquisette, and 2¾ yards of ribbon.

This is perhaps the easiest model in this Service to develop, for once the picoting on the marquisette foundation blouse is done, the two straight, plain seams are made, and the 4-inch hem is in place in the black-satin skirt, the dress may be completed in a very short time. The skirt has two cascade twists of flouncing, each developed from a 2¼-yard length of lace, and the bodice consists of but four little points, each made of a diagonal piece of lace. These are held together on the shoulders with the tiniest of tiny tailored bows made of ¼-inch green-blue and tinsel grosgrain ribbon. A sash of two strands of the ribbon finishes the waist line, tying in a "lover's-knot" bow at the left side front.

And now a word about fans and combs for evening-dress wear. Fans not only are ornate, but give opportunity for unusual color effects in the complete costume. Especially is this true of ostrich-feather fans, for it seems as if they represent every tint and hue, and consequently adapt themselves well to evening gowns. A fan of green-blue, for instance, with the black dress just described, or a deep-orange or an American Beauty one, the ribbon of the dress, of course, matching the fan, would add much to the costume. The comb should harmonize with either the dress or the fan, preferably the latter.

6A

6B

6C

6D

Kimono Panel-Effect Dress

Style.—To say of a well-dressed woman, "She designs all her own frocks and hats," is to compliment her and at the same time pay tribute to a most womanly art. To know how to design distinctive and becoming clothes for oneself is indeed a valuable asset as well as a delightful accomplishment. To design successfully means to combine color, line, fabric, and perhaps decoration into a dress so that it will be becoming to the individual, appropriate for the purpose, and entirely harmonious with the mode.

Some think that to design means to draw with pen or pencil a sketch of a dress, but this is not the kind of designing that a good modiste does, for she, like the sculptor, takes actual materials and uses them to exemplify her interpretation of individuality and mode.

New fashions do not become all women and, fortunately, few desire or have opportunity to accept them all, but there is a right expression of fashion for every woman if she seeks it and will hold to her style once she finds it. This does not mean using the same silhouette each season; it means a happy compromise of all extremes. Distinctive dress is always the very essence of simplicity, rarely extreme in any regard; in fact, simplicity is the foundation on which becoming dress must be built.

To find your style and keep it means just this: If you know that your walk, your build, and your size are not in harmony with short skirts, use a tunic skirt, thus acquiring the short-skirt effect by means of the tunic and using the foundation skirt to make the dress becoming to you. If your arms and shoulders are heavy, just forget that fashion's calendar carries kimono sleeves; they are not for you. Instead, use as narrow a shoulder as the mode will permit. If your back is broad, use a form of panel that will be in accord with other lines in your dress and at the same time lessen the appearance of width.

To study the evolution of fashion is to know that every season offers some form of set-in sleeve, some form of kimono or raglan sleeve, some form of panel, and some form of tunic or overskirt effect, for these have become factors in dress just as waists, sleeves, and skirts have. Fashions revolve on one of our greatest commercial wheels and must, because of their dominant place in trade, lend themselves to individual interpretation and need.

The panel-effect dress shown here, for instance, could have either kimono or set-in sleeves, and it could have knife-plaited sections in place of the loose front panels if more width in the skirt were desired. The waist line could be fitted a trifle more snugly, if the mode required it, without interfering to any great degree with the becomingness of the dress.

Material and Pattern.—Chiffon taffeta of the very softest quality obtainable was chosen in a rather deep shade of golden brown for this model, with its interesting looped-under panels. Perhaps the reason for the choice of taffeta was that it lends itself so well to plaitings. Besides, there is a suggestion of youthfulness in taffeta that is difficult to resist. For developing such a model for the average figure, 5 yards of taffeta will be required.

McCall pattern No. 9403 may be used as a guide in cutting the foundation skirt and the kimono waist and front panel. In developing the muslin model, make the full-length back panel and the inserted front panels of a becoming width. Cut these panels long enough to loop under the skirt hem in a loose, easy manner.

Observe the neck line and fit it to give you a line that you know to be becoming. If you have not cut the muslin model high enough at the neck, build it up with a piecing. Also, do not hesitate to add a roll or a high collar if it will make the style more becoming. A point always well to consider in connection with neck lines is the shape of hat that you will wear. High neck lines call for hats that are inclined to a compact outline, while low neck lines or those finished with lace and soft materials harmonize with a hat of finer texture and lacy or feathery construction.

Although the high collar has a distinct place in present-day styles, the collarless neck line has by no means been abandoned for it. But for the person having a long slender neck that is not enchanced by a collarless effect, the advisability of providing a high collar should not be overlooked whenever the design as a whole will permit such a change. For instance, this style would appear well balanced with a high crushed collar finished in kerchief effect, similar to that shown in one of the suits illustrated elsewhere in this Service. Or, if a fitted high collar were employed, it might be finished with a plaiting at the upper edge. In such a case, the plaiting at the waist line should be eliminated, for otherwise the trimming would appear overdone.

Before removing the muslin model, determine whether a narrow or a wide plaiting should be used to define the upper edge of the girdle or, if the figure is short-waisted, whether the plaiting unfavorably emphasizes the waist line and should, therefore, be omitted. Long-waisted figures will usually find the plaiting becoming.

Construction.—First of all, prepare the strips for the plaiting. Plan to have the plaitings for the sides about 5 inches wide and those for the waist line of the width you decided on in the development of the muslin model. Then have the material hemstitched so that it may be cut to form a picoted edge for the plaiting. Join the strips with narrow French fells and provide a length that is three times as great as that required in the finished plaiting. Have the plaiting done by a firm that makes a specialty of this work.

Secure the plaitings in the side skirt seams when joining the gores, and in order to provide a placket opening leave the left seam open at the top, turn under the front edge of the opening, and baste the plaiting flat to this. Then finish the opening with a continuous placket.

To prepare for the application of the front skirt panels, baste over each point indicated for the slashes a narrow strip of silk that is about 1 inch longer than the slash is desired. Stitch ⅛ inch each side of the line marked for the slash, graduating the width of this stitching to almost nothing at the ends. Then cut the opening, turn the applied strip directly on the seam line to the wrong side of the skirt, and baste the edges to hold them in this manner. Gather the ends of the front skirt panels, which have been picot-edged, insert them in the openings, and stitch around the openings close to the turned edge. The under edge should, of course, be stitched free from the panel.

Secure the side body and sleeve sections of the waist to the lining. Then apply the front and back panels, which have been finished with picoting, and arrange for the opening on the left shoulder and at the left side front. For a sleeve finish, have the lower edge picoted.

Attach the waist and skirt to an inside stay belt and finish the portion of the waist line of the skirt that extends from the side opening of the waist to the skirt placket, in order that this may be left free from the belt and secured in position by means of snap fasteners after the belt is hooked. Tack the girdle in position, so that it may be looped at the center back after the closing of the remainder of the dress has been arranged. Then, in finishing the dress, secure the loose panels to the lower edge of the skirt as previously directed.

Model 8

Variations of Kimono Panel-Effect Dress

Designers of clothes may be likened to a singing chorus. Each one sings according to his own powers of interpretation, but first he must have the right key to fashion, just as to the song, and then beauty will be expressed according to the degree of feeling, individuality, and training. Sometimes Nature provides a beautiful voice that needs no training, just as it sometimes makes a modiste genius. But such instances are very unusual. Training is the permanent, constructive way. The more study, training, and practice, the more delightful will be the expression and the more perfect the product.

First, find the key to fashions, and then design every note as perfectly as your skill will allow. Artistic, becoming clothes are the true expression of beauty-loving and comprehensive thought, and every woman can, by cultivation, express beauty, the heritage of the age, to some degree. The prominent place that women occupy in business, political, and social life makes becoming clothes, right clothes, and careful grooming totally essential. "Good dressing like genius is the capacity for taking infinite pains."

Model 8A.—This silhouette, smart and much favored, may be achieved in many ways. It may be developed in different materials, proving a good design for silk, as well as cloth. Serge, tricotine, satin, faille, and silk poplin are materials from which selection may be made for this type of dress. The trimming, in addition to the decorative stitches, may be of satin, Hercules braid, or ribbon. For instance, on a cloth dress, satin, braid, or ribbon should be used as trimming. In case braid or ribbon is selected, loops 1¼ to 1¾ inches long should be made to serve for the eight ornamental drops on each side of the front. If the material is satin or heavy faille, then the trimming should be of self-material, allowing the richness of the material to suffice.

Should light-weight faille or silk poplin be used for the development of this model, the material should be cut so that the crosswise threads run lengthwise of the dress. With these lighter-weight materials, dainty lace or fine net may be used for collar and cuffs, and a fitted facing may be applied to all panel effects and the sleeve and waist-line edges, this being held in place with two or three rows of darning-stitches or two rows of plain glove-stitching in self or contrasting color.

The knife plaits of the back and sides of the skirt form a popular and pleasing method of adding fulness and still retaining the straight silhouette. They may be replaced, however, with a straight foundation skirt having a panel formed by means of plaits to continue the lines of the back waist and to give a full-length effect to the panel; or, if desired, a panel may be cut to hang from the neck to the hem. If the material available does not give sufficient length for the full-length panel, a plain seam may be used to join two lengths, but the joining must be planned accurately, so that the seam will come directly under the narrow belt. For such a joining, a plain seam should be used and this carefully pressed open to make it as inconspicuous as possible. Seams are not objectionable, and frequently they can be placed to good advantage in a dress and serve as a construction feature rather than a necessary piecing.

Model 8B.—Simplicity is happily evident in this model, the ribbon rosettes serving as the only decoration, and even these may be omitted if the material in itself is beautiful enough to need no decoration or a material with a design is used. On the other hand, a braiding or embroidery design may be substituted for the ribbon rosettes if desired.

The foundation skirt is of the regulation two-piece type made of two lengths of material slightly gored over the hips and at the waist. The tunic is a straight length of the material, hemmed on each front edge and at the bottom for a finish. The edges of the panel of the front and back waist portions may be picoted or faced back with a fitted facing of the material.

If embroidery is substituted for the ribbon rosettes, the space occupied by the design should be smaller. In addition to the embroidery, the edges of the waist panel, waist line, and sleeves may be finished by turning the material back ½ inch and pressing it and then holding it in place with two rows of darning-stitches done in silk floss to match that used for the skirt designs.

Model 8C.—The adaptability of panels is reason for their seeming ever the vogue. Some say they have had panels and want something different, but panels in one form or another, like tunic effects, are here, it seems, to stay. At least one panel dress can be found in the wardrobe of every woman who is at all inclined to stoutness and who has made a definite study of individually becoming lines in dress.

The panels in the skirt of this model give the appearance of length to the front, so this type of dress, even with its cascaded sides, could be worn by one medium large, provided the soutache braid were used to decorate the waist panels instead of the sleeves, for then it would tend to reduce the width through the shoulders. When this is done, the back panel should extend up far enough to make a turn-over collar of 1½ to 2¾ inches.

The original of this dress was developed in smoke crêpe meteor, with dark-brown soutache braid, its unusualness in color combination adding to its attractiveness. Navy-blue crêpe meteor with the design done with gray or beaver-colored wool is also an effective combination, especially if a plaited neck frill of tulle or Georgette in harmonizing color is available for wear with the dress.

Model 8D.—Plaids seem always to express youthfulness and to call for simplicity in design. Both of these points are especially evident in this model. The skirt of the original is of darkest-green serge, with plaid of navy, brown, lighter green, and cream, while the bodice is of plain green crêpe meteor that is a trifle darker in shade than the green of the skirt.

The bodice may be made long-waisted in effect and may have set-in sleeves if they are more becoming. The narrow wrist bands and the back of the stand-up, true-bias collar are faced with the plaid material of the skirt, these suggesting the connection of blouse and skirt. Buttons covered with the plaid material may also be used in preference to those covered with the material of the blouse. If desired, a Tuxedo-collar effect of plaid may be used to divide the front and bring the collar closer to the neck.

The knife plaits of the skirt are arranged in sections, so as both to avoid overmuch fulness in the skirt and to give the panel effect by means of the plain spaces. A narrow bias band of the blouse material finished with a flat bow serves to cover the joining of the blouse and the skirt.

This style of blouse is an excellent one to finish by itself for wear with separate skirts. Blouses for wear with suits continue to come over the skirt and form their own waist-line finish. Many of the dress materials are used for overblouses, satin, duvetyn, chiffon, and various silk-crêpe weaves being prominent in the showings. Figured silks prove smart and attractive if they are worn with plaited skirts of plain material.

Practically the only type of "tuck-in" blouse that is receiving very much attention is the hand-made variety in soft, sheer white materials, such as batiste, voile, and fine lawn. There is an appearance of freshness and daintiness in these hand-made blouses that is quite irresistible, and although shop prices of the very desirable models are, in some cases, prohibitive, the woman who enjoys doing hand work and has time to execute it properly has a means of overcoming this handicap. As the design of most of the hand-made blouses is very plain, they depend almost wholly on odd arrangement of rows of hemstitching for their distinctiveness.

8D

8B

8C

8A

Magic Pattern: *Sleeved Cape*

This is an original Magic Pattern, a project you cut out using diagrams instead of pattern pieces. These were first created by Mary Brooks Picken for the Woman's Institute's student magazines, Inspiration and Fashion Service. My book **Vintage Notions: An Inspirational Guide to Needlework, Cooking, Sewing, Fashion & Fun** *featured 12 original Magic Patterns. Recently I have created modern patterns that were inspired by these vintage gems featured in the book* **The Magic Pattern Book**, *which I licensed with Workman Publishing. We have chosen to keep the authenticity of this original pattern intact and therefore have not changed instructions based on modern fabrics and techniques. Note at the end of this pattern you will find helpful tips for drafting pattern pieces.*

▶▶▶HOW OFTEN have you sat playing bridge or canasta, or in a movie, and wished you had something to put over your shoulders, something that would not slip off, that would look attractive with whatever dress you were wearing, be easy to handle, and have just enough warmth for comfort?

A sleeved cape of fake fur is ideal for the purposes mentioned. If of a conservative color, it can be worn through spring and summer with suits and dresses.

Sleeved cape illustrated was made from ⅞ yd. of 54-in. fake fur.

For the cuffs tear a crosswise strip 4½ in. deep and the full width of 54-in. fabric. Divide this evenly into four pieces, each slightly more than 13 in. Place right sides of two of these pieces together; seam two crosswise edges and across one end. Turn right side out.

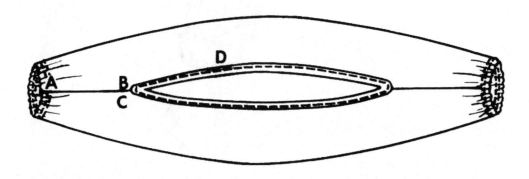

Seam ends of cape piece up from selvages a distance of about 10 in., as A to B in diagram. Turn right side out. Gather across bottom of each sleeve at selvage as at A; then put cuffs on, making them the size you like them. They are large enough for ends to extend out about 2 in. as illustration shows.

Finish neck and bottom edges with 3/8-in. grosgrain ribbon, as at D. Stitch this ribbon to the raw edge, lapping a scant 1/4 in.; then slip-stitch free edge of ribbon to fabric.

Two brilliant buttons added to each cuff can dress this cape up and help make it gay for evening. Cape color may be bright red, royal blue, silver gray, black, or what you choose.

Your Measurement Chart & Notes on Making Magic Patterns

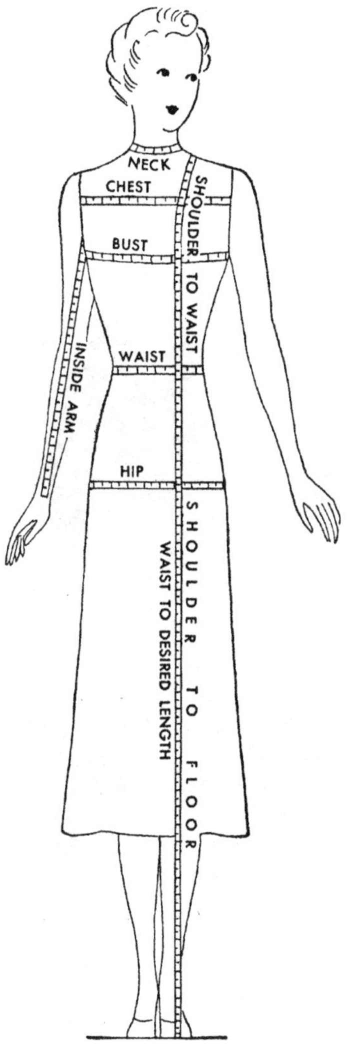

BUST (Fullest Part)............._____

WAIST ...._____

HIP (Fullest Part) ...._____

WIDTH OF CHEST............_____

FRONT WAIST LENGTH
Shoulder to Waist............._____

FRONT SKIRT LENGTH
Waist to Desired Length........_____

FRONT FULL LENGTH
Shoulder to Floor ...._____

NECK (At Base) ...._____

SHOULDER
Neck to Armhole Line.........._____

ARMHOLE ...._____

WIDTH OF BACK ...._____

BACK LENGTH
Neck to Waist ...._____

BACK LENGTH
Neck to Floor................_____

OUTSIDE ARM
Shoulder to Wrist (Arm Bent)...._____

INSIDE ARM
Armhole to Wrist (Arm Straight).._____

UPPER ARM (Fullest Part)......._____

ELBOW (Arm Bent) ...._____

WRIST ...._____

HAND (Closed) ...._____

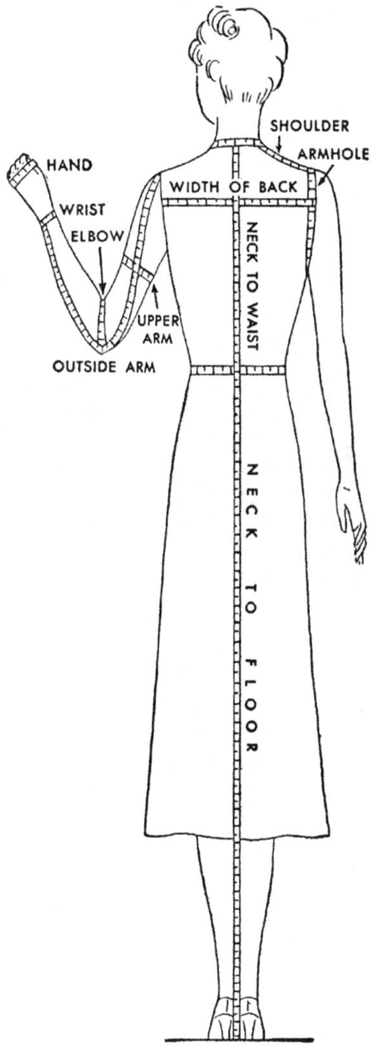

Keep Accurate Measurements

Since the garments in this book are all cut from measurements, it is necessary to have accurate ones to follow. Keep a list of your own measurements always at hand for ready reference.

Measurements for fitted garments should be taken over the type of foundation garments you expect to wear with them. Remove dress, jacket, or coat, which would distort the measurements. Do not take measurements too tight. Make all easy enough for comfort. The chart shows how to place the tape correctly for each measurement.

Making The Pattern

If you have the least doubt about your ability to chalk out the garment on your fabric, then rough it out first with crayon or heavy pencil on wrapping paper or newspaper. Cut out the paper pattern and use it to cut your garment. Cutting from a diagram, you can be sure that the proportions are correct for your size and that the garment will be a good fit.

From Noon to Midnight

A Domestic Play in Eight Scenes—With a Happy Ending

Scene One

Scene Two

Scene One—1 P. M.

(Telephone rings. Mrs. Ellis answers)

Margaret Ellis: "Hello! Yes, this is Margaret. Oh, hello Ruth. Fine! Tonight? A dinner party? Why, we'd love to come! Who's going to be there? How lovely! Yes, indeed, Bob and I will surely come. Seven o'clock? Thank you so much. Good-bye until tonight."

Scene Two—1.30 P. M.

Margaret: "Now I said we'd go, but what shall I wear? I won't wear that blue again. I know! I'll go down town this minute and get something for a new dress and have it all made before Bob gets home. Thanks to my Institute Course, I can do it easily."

Scene Three—2 P. M.

Margaret: "What beautiful materials! Brown— Bob likes that best and it *is* so becoming. Let's see, I'll need just two yards of this lovely velvet and it's only $3.50 a yard, a half-yard of metallic cloth will be $3.25, and six yards of ribbon will cost only $1.20. Altogether that will be $11.45 and I will have a truly beautiful dress that would cost at least $40 ready made. Won't Bob be surprised?"

Scene Four—3 P. M.

Margaret: "It certainly is easy to cut out this dress. Only four measurements to take. Here it is all cut out in ten minutes without needing a pattern. Thirty minutes more and the blouse seams are sewed together. Four twenty-five and the neck and sleeves are bound and the metallic cloth joined in the skirt. Now all I have to do is to sew the skirt and blouse together and drop the ribbon over the shoulders."

Scene Five—5 P. M.

Margaret: "Finished in two hours! And doesn't it fit beautifully? When Bob first sees it he'll think I've bought an expensive dress that we really can't afford. But when I tell him I made it myself this afternoon and that it all cost was $11.45, well, I wonder what he'll say then. Guess I'll go upstairs and get some beauty sleep before he comes home."

Scene Six—6.30 P. M.

Bob: "Are you sure you're not fibbing, Margaret? Do you actually mean to tell me that you, yourself, *made* this gorgeous creation in two hours and that it cost only $11.45?"

Margaret: "Yes, dear, it's all true. Why, it isn't work at all to make lovely clothes by the new method I learned from the Woman's Institute. I enjoy it more than anything— except wearing the clothes and hearing your praises?"

Scene Seven—7 P. M.

Ruth Johnson, the Hostess: "Margaret, how *stunning* you look! I don't like to be personal, but I didn't know you could get dresses as handsome as that one anywhere in this town. Did it come from New York?"

Margaret (shyly): "I'm glad you like it."

Ruth: "Like it! Why, my dear, it's the best-looking gown I've seen this season, and it fits you perfectly!"

Scene Eight—Back Home

Bob: "Well, Margaret, I do believe I have the cleverest wife in seven states! The way every one admired you! I was never so proud of you in all my life."

Margaret: "Don't congratulate me, Bob. Remember I couldn't sew at all a few months ago. Any woman can easily learn through the Woman's Institute to do what I did this afternoon."

Scene Three

Scene Four

Scene Five

Scene Six

Scene Eight

Scene Seven

Wouldn't you like to have frocks like these? Every one of these dresses was designed by the Woman's Institute, and every dressmaking student was furnished with complete instructions for making them in the shortest possible time. This is just one exclusive feature of the Institute's fascinating new plan and service

It Seems Too Good To Be True

—Yet thousands of women have learned—right in their own homes—in spare time—by this new plan— to make the lovely clothes they have always wanted

FROM now on—you need never again pay high prices for your clothes. From now on—you need never worry about not having all the pretty dresses your heart desires.

From now on—you need never envy the woman who knows how to sew. From now on—you can never say that sewing is hard or tedious or uninteresting.

For a new method has been created by which the planning and making of lovely frocks that will inspire the admiration of all your friends can be a fascinating joy to you. And it is so easy, so simple that you can have the clothes you have longed for and dreamed about almost at once.

It was inevitable that some time a new fascinating way to make clothes would be found. And who could possibly have developed it so well as the Woman's Institute? For the Institute has taught more women to sew than any other school in the world. More than 200,000 women and girls have learned or are learning to make their own clothes through its fascinating method.

These women are of all ages from schoolgirls to grandmothers. They are found in every stage of society from the palatial home on Riverside Drive to the lonely ranch house on a western prairie. They represent every degree of education from the cultured wives and daughters of college presidents to women of foreign birth, with only a meager knowledge of our language and customs.

There are more than 130,000 home women who study in spare afternoon and evening hours, 26,000 business and professional women who learn at home in the evening, 8,000 teachers and schoolgirls, and thousands of others in every conceivable occupation who turn their spare moments of day and evening to profit by learning to design and make pretty things to wear.

Making Clothes Now "a Positive Joy"

And while we have been helping these thousands, we have been working constantly on new methods to still further simplify dressmaking, to make a joy out of what used to be a tedious task.

Today students of the Institute are learning with such ease and such amazing success that letters are pouring in on us telling of their happiness and appreciation.

"I just wish I could begin to tell you the happiness this course has brought me," writes Mrs.

Originally published in "How You Can Have More and Prettier Clothes" Book, 1925

Roser of Detroit, Mich. "I am now making all the clothes for my mother, my baby and myself. And far from being a task, it is the pleasantest occupation I know of. I find it a positive joy."

"To me," writes Mrs. Nourse, from Gold Hill, Oregon, "this is the most fascinating subject I ever studied. Already people remark about the individuality of my clothes."

"Fun Instead of Work"

From Winchester, N. H., Miss Helen E. Thompson writes, "I just love to study. It is fun instead of work. Everything is so clear. I don't see how one could help but understand."

"I wish I could find words to express my appreciation," writes Mrs. Burton Read from Tisdale, Saskatchewan. "The best I can do is to recommend the Institute wherever I go and advertise it by the clothes I wear."

From the heart of New York City Mrs. Evelyn Dalal writes, "I find it the most fascinating thing I have ever undertaken—a pleasure, not a task, it is so interesting."

And Miss Nora Holcomb sends this word, "The course keeps on being so interesting—it has far exceeded all my expectations."

Could you ask more convincing proof than these messages from all sections of the country that the Institute's method really makes dressmaking a delightful pleasure?

New Clothes At Once

What does this new development mean to you? It means that now you really can start at once and make with your own hands all the lovely clothes you want.

It means you can receive an invitation to some social affair at noon and go that very evening in a charming new frock that will surprise all your friends.

It means that now you can be complimented and admired for having a wonderful wardrobe of attractive clothes—dresses, wraps, everything at what you would have to pay for one or two ordinary garments ready made.

Earn Money If You Wish

It means more joy in your life than you ever thought possible. For the planning and making of your own clothes by this new plan is so easy, so fascinating, so much fun that you will want to spend every spare moment at your new-found accomplishment. And if you wish, you can speedily acquire such skill that you can go into business as a dressmaker—you can plan and make clothes for others in your own home or have a shop of your own.

No matter how many times you have thought about learning dressmaking and given it up, surely now nothing must stand in the way of your beginning at once on this new and wonderful plan.

Miss Agnes M. Stout
Elizabeth, N. J.

Miss Lillian B. Wood
San Francisco, Calif.

Miss Ethel M. Haselton
Westbrook, Me

Mrs. Katherine Gannon
Providence, R. I.

Here are just four typical students of the Institute. Wouldn't you like to join with women and girls like these and know the happiness of having more and prettier clothes at a third their usual cost?

"I cannot say enough in praise of your courses," writes Miss Ethel M. Haselton, Westbrook, Maine. "I know of no one thing in my life which has brought me more happiness, to say nothing of the money I have saved by being able to sew for myself, and the money I have earned by sewing for others in my spare time."

You Learn Right In Your Own Home
—No Matter Where You Live

NINE years ago you might have doubted your own ability to learn at home, from a teacher a hundred or a thousand miles away, to make beautiful distinctive clothes. But the success of the Woman's Institute in these last nine years has swept away every reason for such a doubt. And the success of thousands upon thousands of women of all ages, in all circumstances, and living in all parts of the world has demonstrated not only that you *can* learn at home but that the Institute's method is the *easiest*, the *quickest*, the *most satisfactory*, and the *least expensive* plan by which a knowledge of dressmaking can be acquired.

Since all the instruction is carried on by correspondence, the advantages of the Institute are open to women everywhere the mails reach. So there are today students of the Woman's Institute in practically every city, town, and community from Maine to California. There are 10,200 in California, there are 7,300 in Texas, 12,950 in Ohio, 18,600 in the New England States. In Canada, there are more than 9,000 and in practically every foreign country you will find women learning how to make pretty clothes through the Woman's Institute. So wherever you may live there are probably students of the Woman's Institute living near you.

Consider the advantages of learning at home by this new plan. It makes your own home the schoolroom. It makes the hours of study whatever hours you may have to spare from your household duties or occupation. It supplies you with textbooks especially prepared for individual study in the home. And it supplements these books with *personal instruction* by correspondence so intimate and helpful and given with such understanding that you feel the constant inspiring presence of the Instructor at your side.

And after all, home is the natural place to learn dressmaking. Sewing is an accomplishment of and for the home. Your tools are at hand, your mind is at ease, you study in an atmosphere of pleasant, familiar home surroundings. You do not necessarily have to interfere in any way with your present work or your social duties. You simply fit your study plan to your own convenience. And whatever your circumstances — wherever you live, in city, town, or country, the Woman's Institute *comes to you*, bringing its message of practical information and personal inspiration and help.

Just Like Going to School at Home

One of my friends asked me one day why I did not study sewing. I said that I would jump at the chance if I could find a teacher, but that was impossible in the small town in which we lived.

After joining the Institute and receiving my first lessons, I was completely won and sat up far into the night to study, though it does not seem like studying; it is so interesting. The lessons are all so clear anyone can understand them, and really it is just like going to school, with this advantage—one can study just when one chooses.

Mrs. Ruth P. Willis, Villa Rica, Ga.

Originally published in "How You Can Have More and Prettier Clothes" Book, 1925

Why Pay for Anything But Materials?

WOULD you like to be able to save one-half or two-thirds of the money you now spend for clothes? Would you like to have two or three times as many dresses and other garments, and even prettier and more becoming ones, at no increased expense to you? You can!

Suppose you see a pretty dress on display in a store, price at $40. How much of that $40 could you save? Let us see. You can go to the piece-goods department of the same store and buy goods, trimmings, every item of material necessary to make the same dress for $12 to $15. What makes up the other $25 or $28? The manufacturer bought the goods. Then he paid garment workers to make them up. Then he added a profit and sold the dress to a jobber, who added his profit and sold it to the retailer, who added still another profit and sold it to you.

By the time a dress or any garment reaches you, the cost of the materials represents a relatively small part of the retail price. Yet the cost of the materials is all you ever need pay for your clothes when you make them yourself. No matter what the garment, the same thing holds true. On a suit costing $60 at retail, you can easily save $35 by making it; on a dress or skirt retailing at $15 you can save $8 or $10; even on a blouse or simple home dress selling as low as $4 you can save $2 or more by buying the materials and making it yourself.

The chart illustrated on this page shows you perhaps more plainly than words, just what proportion of the cost you can save on every garment you wear. Why should *you* pay for labor, when you can so easily do the work yourself? Why should *you* pay for someone else's profit, when you can, if you wish, earn that profit *for yourself?*

How much do you now spend on clothes for yourself and your family in a year? Think what it would mean to you to be able to save half or two-thirds of that amount. Think of the other comforts or luxuries you or your family could enjoy or the money you could put away against a rainy day. Think how it would simplify your home problems, what a load it would take off your shoulders, what a genuine help it would be to be able to make all your own clothes at such savings.

You Can Have More and Finer Clothes for the Money You Now Spend

If your present dress allowance is well within what you can afford, then you can have twice as many pretty clothes by spending your money only

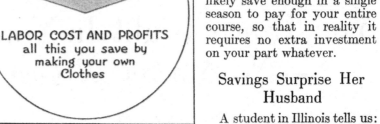

for materials. You can add to your wardrobe those extra garments that will provide you with a pleasing variety of everything. When you attend social functions, you will be able to select from several becoming afternoon or evening gowns instead of having only one to wear. When dressing for the street, a number of suits or dresses will await your choosing.

A member in Massachusetts writes: "I have more pretty dresses than I ever had at any time in my life. Just think, six summer dresses and two new hats—and last summer I really shed tears for want of one decent dress. My children all have nice clothes and sewing is a pleasure instead of a burden now."

Surely you see the great advantage that these savings or this greater value for your money will mean. Do not let the cost of a course delay you. If you spend only an average amount for clothes you will likely save enough in a single season to pay for your entire course, so that in reality it requires no extra investment on your part whatever.

Savings Surprise Her Husband

A student in Illinois tells us: "The money I paid for my course is all repaid. In fact I have earned twice as much. I have made all the clothes this year for myself and the children and many for others. My husband was surprised to see all I had made and how much I had saved."

Remember, the benefits are not something you must wait weeks or months to realize. Your course will be practical and helpful from the very start. As soon as you have made just a few simple garments you will be so surprised and pleased with your work and the money you have saved that you will be sorry you did not join the Institute months before.

"I have saved the cost of the Dressmaking and Millinery Courses three times over on clothes for myself and my mother," writes one student, "and I now dress better on $150 a year than I did on $275 before, when I went to a very good dressmaker. My principal savings this year have been on a beautiful braided coat copied from a model priced at $90, which cost me $20, and a cream gabardine suit which cost me $31 while the original was priced at $75. Then I have a navy costume, which looks like a new one and worth $50, but was made at a cost of $15 from a four-year old green striped suit, which I dyed. My father thought me wildly extravagant when I decided to take the Course, and I often laugh to myself now, when I hear him singing the praises of the Institute to every one."

Originally published in "How You Can Have More and Prettier Clothes" Book, 1925

Every Season You Can Be Admired By All Your Friends

PERHAPS you have been through the humiliating experience of having to make some of your clothes "do," after they have gone out of style. Possibly you have met friends on the street or at a social affair and keenly felt the difference between their smart new clothes and those you were still wearing.

It does seem a shame the way fashions change so quickly. The lovely dress of today is out of style all too soon. But there is nothing you can do to stop style changes. It is the natural result of competition among the designers. Each is constantly endeavoring to create new ideas in dress that will catch woman's fancy. And some of these ideas are always accepted and become the vogue. That is why, with each succeeding season, the styles change so radically—so completely. That is why a woman who wears last year's clothes sometimes looks as definitely out of fashion as if she wore the clothes of five years ago.

But now you need *never* look out of date. You need *never* wear clothes of last year's style. You need *never* wear a makeshift of any kind. Indeed, you can now appear, every season, in the smartest, up-to-the-minute fashions. As soon as any of your dresses, suits, or wraps begin to go out of style, you can remodel them cleverly into the new fashion. And, since you will need to pay only for materials, you will be able to make a smart new costume whenever you want it. Whenever a new

type of dress or wrap becomes the mode, you can at once create one for yourself in a few hours' time, in the colors and fabrics that are most becoming and for a third of its cost in the stores.

The Joy of Being Well Dressed

Think of the feeling of pride and satisfaction that can be yours when you realize that *every season* you can have the variety of smart, distinctive, becoming clothes which will put you definitely in the class of the best-dressed women in your town. Think of being able to achieve that distinction at an expenditure so low that you, yourself, will be amazed at it. Think of the new joy in life that can be yours—the rightful, womanly joy of being beautifully and appropriately dressed at all times. And think of being able to achieve that result by the most pleasurable and fascinating occupation you can imagine!

Wherever you go—at any time—morning, afternoon, or evening—whether it is merely a simple home breakfast, a company luncheon, a social or business meeting in the afternoon, an every-day dinner in your own home or a formal dinner party at the home of a socially prominent family of your town—you can always go with the assurance that you are attractively, fashionably, and appropriately dressed. And this means that you will be admired by all your friends.

Originally published in "How You Can Have More and Prettier Clothes" Book, 1925

Here are actual photographs of three charming dresses made by Miss Marion Kemp, a nineteen-year-old graduate of the Institute. And each of them was made in less than an afternoon. Surely you could find no smarter frocks in the most exclusive shop. Before enrolling Miss Kemp could do only the simplest plain sewing.

You Can Design and Make Clothes That Express Your Personality

WHAT is your impression of any woman the first time you see her? Is it not invariably an impression of her clothes? Human nature is a curious thing. It forms such definite conclusions from first impressions. And how difficult it is, afterwards, to change those first impressions!

Think of how many people see you every year—every week—who judge you entirely by your appearance. They do not know anything about your character or your ability or your disposition. They can judge you only by the way you look—by the impression your clothes make.

What Do Your Clothes Tell Others About You?

Your clothes are the message you send to others *about yourself*. Even your friends and relatives—the people who know you well—cannot help being influenced in their opinion of you by the way you look. You may be ever so clever, ever so capable, ever so sweet, but why not let your

clothes *bring out* these lovely traits of your personality instead of submerging them?

To do this you should have clothes distinctively becoming, clothes that appropriately frame your beauty, clothes that accentuate your charm, clothes that overcome any plainness or little defect of feature or figure—in short, clothes that express your own individuality and invariably convey the impression of having been designed, planned, and made just for you.

Clothes That Never Look "Home-Made"

Through your Institute course you will learn to completely make any garment that your fancy may desire—a waist, a skirt, a piece of lingerie, a smart dress, an evening gown, a suit—and, you can acquire such skill that nothing you produce will ever appear "home-made," but will, on the contrary, give every impression of having come from the exclusive shop of some fashionable dressmaker. So when a dress is finished and you stand before your mirror or wear it among your

Originally published in "How You Can Have More and Prettier Clothes" Book, 1925

friends you will experience that deep sense of satisfaction that you are dressed correctly and appropriately.

The secret of this skill lies in the fact that the Institute helps you, first of all, to understand yourself, to know your type. Then it tells you what lines to follow, what colors to use, what materials to select to dress your type with distinction. It teaches you how to design and how to make garments that are in every sense an expression of your individuality.

In giving you this understanding of the true principles of distinctive dress, the Institute will teach you how to study and understand style, so that you will always know what is correct and becoming, no matter what changes the fashions of each new season may bring forth. You will understand the cycles in which fashions move, the principles underlying all styles, and you will be able to *interpret* each season's fashion tendencies in developing your own clothes.

This means that you will be able to create for yourself designs that will be thoroughly smart and yet will be distinctive from any dress or suit you will see wherever you may go. You need never again experience the embarrassment of meeting someone in a dress or suit "just like yours," or in having your clothes branded as "ordinary" or unbecoming.

Here is a modish ensemble suit of lovely charmeen, especially becoming to the young woman for whom it was made. It actually cost less than $25 to make, yet it could not be duplicated in the shops for $60.

What Designing Really Means

To design successfully means to combine color, line, fabric, and perhaps decoration into a dress so that it will be becoming to the individual, appropriate for the purpose, and entirely harmonious with the mode. Some think that to design means to draw with pen or pencil a sketch of a dress, but this is not the kind of designing that a good modiste does, for she, like the sculptor, takes actual materials and uses them to exemplify in the gown she creates her interpretation of individuality and mode.

To find the style that fits your *personality* and *individuality* means just this: If you know that your walk, your build, and your size are not in harmony with the longer skirts, use a short skirt, acquiring the longer effect by means of long panels and drapes and depending on the foundation skirt to make the dress becoming. If your arms and shoulders are heavy, just forget that fashion's

calendar carries kimono sleeves; they are not for you. Use instead as narrow a shoulder as the mode will permit. If your back is broad, use a form of panel that will be in accord with other lines in your dress and at the same time tend to lessen the appearance of width.

If you study the evolution of fashion you will learn that every season offers some form of set-in sleeve, some form of kimono or raglan sleeve, some form of panel, and some form of tunic or overskirt effect, for these have become factors in dress, just as waists and skirts.

Do you not begin to see already, just from these few suggestions, how fascinating the study of dress can be when you consider it in its relation to your own individuality or the individuality of others? What could be more delightful than to study the season's fashions, the new materials, the prevailing colors, always in their application to your particular type?

Distinctive Clothes for You

As you come to *know* yourself in a dress sense and to understand color, line, and fabric, a new world of ideas will take shape in your mind. You will begin to plan costumes in which every line and touch emphasize your own charm, dresses both correct and distinctively becoming. This is designing in its truest sense.

A young woman who is studying with the Institute writes that her lessons have given her the definite secrets that underlie all designing. "I learned as a girl to sew at home," she says, "but always with a consciousness of something lacking in the style which, try as I would, I could not obtain. Thanks to the Institute, I have learned that subtle, indefinable difference between the clothes I *could* make and those I *wanted* to make. I enjoy a look into the mirror better these days than in the old ones."

Does it seem almost too good to be true—to be able to create for yourself, for your children, for your friends, stylish, distinctive, becoming clothes? Is it hard to realize that this skill you have always wanted is so easily to be gained in your own home? Thousands upon thousands of Institute members have swept away every doubt. The Woman's Institute has made it possible for every woman to dress herself becomingly and distinctively for one-third to one-half of what she has been spending.

Originally published in "How You Can Have More and Prettier Clothes" Book, 1925

You Will Be Able to Copy or Adapt Any Attractive Garment You See

—and at less than half what it would cost you to buy it!

TO many women, the fact that they can learn to copy any garment they happen to see and admire is one of the most attractive features of the course. Think what this ability may mean to you. Think how often, at the theater, at church, at tea, at a dance, you see some stunning gown that you admire very much. Or you may see it in a shop window, or in a fashion magazine. How you wish you might have one like it! But you know that the cost would be prohibitive. Even if you were to tell y o u r dressmaker about it, you would probably be unable to remember all the details, and the result would fall far short of the desired effect. And to buy it in the shops would certainly be an unwarranted extravagance.

But the Woman's Institute Course will show you exactly how to copy these exclusive, h a n d s o m e models and how to adapt them cleverly to your own size and type of figure. So you see, you can really and truly have any gown, suit, wrap, or undergarment that happens to appeal to you—and at no expense for anything but materials—which is anywhere from one-half to one-third of the retail cost of the finished garment—sometimes even less.

Copies $45 Gown For $8

A member out in Washington writes that she saw a dress in a store window that just suited her, priced forty-five dollars. She made a little sketch of the design, bought the materials, and copied the dress down to the last touch of embroidery for

Copies $135 Evening Gown For $22.50

"I had to have an evening dress for a lodge ball. I tried to find a reasonably priced dress in the stores, but the one I liked was $135. Well, that price was out of the question for poor me. So I decided to copy it. I was satisfied as soon as the dress was finished, but imagine my delight when a friend told my husband I was the best dressed woman at the ball! And when a friend from New York City complimented me and refused to believe I had made it or that it cost me only $22.50, my happiness was complete."

MRS. FRANKLIN BEECHER, York, Penna.

exactly eight dollars! When it was done she compared it with the one in the store and she says, "Mine was better material and better made."

When you have learned the fascinating secrets of designing which the Institute makes so clear to you, you will be able to judge every new fashion feature in its relation to your own individuality. New fashions do not become all women, but there is a right expression of each season's fashions for you. To find and develop that expression in the clothes you create is to use the art of designing in its truest sense.

You need never take up some new style in its most e x t r e m e f o r m. Rather you can adapt it, modify it, and use it in such a way that your clothes will be always modish and yet at the same time will accentuate the charm of your own personality. You can have that satisfying sense of knowing that your costume is not only stylish in color and line, but distinctively becoming to you.

For remember our purpose is to teach you to make clothes that are not only beautiful and fashionable but at the same time *distinctively becoming* and appropriate to the person who is to wear them.

This individual interest in *your* particular needs —this taking into account *your* particular type of figure, coloring, etc.—is one of the most wonderful features of the Woman's Institute Course. You are *not* simply one of a large class, all receiving the same instruction, but from the very day you enroll, our constant aim and purpose is to give *you* the intimate *personal* attention which you need.

Originally published in "How You Can Have More and Prettier Clothes" Book, 1925

If you enjoyed this issue of *Inspiration—Vintage Notions Monthly*, visit AmyBarickman.com for my curated collection of vintage content including patterns and books for needle and thread, inspiring fabrics and textiles and free vintage art every Friday. Be sure to tune in to *Vintage Notions* video episodes for a guided tour through my collection of sewing and fashion history, as well as modern projects inspired by my extensive library.

www.amybarickman.com
Find free images, inspiration and books for the sewing and needle arts!

www.indygojunction.com
Featuring digital & print patterns, books, tutorials, giveaways, project ideas, & more!

Subscribe to each of our eNewsletters to learn about new products, receive special offers, discounts, videos, and get a FREE eBook!

Inspiration Vintage Notions Monthly , Volume 1, Issue 2 (VN0102)

For wholesale ordering information contact Amy Barickman, LLC at 913.341.5559 or amyb@amybarickman.com, P.O. Box 30238, Kansas City, MO 64112

CPSIA information can be obtained
at www.ICGtesting.com
Printed in the USA
LVOW05s0830191216

517917LV00016B/639/P